Acting Up

Acting Up

Me, Myself & *Irene*

LYNNE McGRANGER
WITH SUMMER LAND

JB

First published in Australia in 2021 by Echo
This edition published in the UK in 2021 by John Blake Publishing
an imprint of Bonnier Books UK
4th Floor, Victoria House
Bloomsbury Square,
London, WC1B 4DA
England

Owned by Bonnier Books
Sveavägen 56, Stockholm, Sweden

www.facebook.com/johnblakebooks
twitter.com/jblakebooks

Hardback ISBN: 978-1-78946-533-4
Ebook ISBN: 978-1-78946-534-1

British Library Cataloguing-in-Publication Data:

A catalogue record for this book is available from the British Library.

Cast shot of *Home and Away* and photo from *Dancing with the Stars* courtesy
of Channel 7. All other photographs courtesy of the author.

Some names and identifying details in this book have been changed to protect the
privacy of individuals. Where names have been changed, any likeness to a person by that
name is purely coincidental.

Typeset by Shaun Jury

Printed and bound in Great Britain by Clays Ltd, Elcograf S.p.A.

1 3 5 7 9 10 8 6 4 2

Every reasonable effort has been made to trace copyright-holders of material
reproduced in this book, but if any have been inadvertently overlooked the publishers
would be glad to hear from them.

John Blake Publishing is an imprint of Bonnier Books UK
www.bonnierbooks.co.uk

For Paul and Clancy, with endless love

Contents

Foreword   ix

Chapter 1   A (Soap) Star is Born   1

Chapter 2   Eating for Australia   15

Chapter 3   Are You There, God? It's Me, Lynne   27

Chapter 4   Seventeen Going on Ten   39

Chapter 5   Bye Bye Blakehurst, Hello Wagga   51

Chapter 6   Adulting Away and at Home   71

Chapter 7   Back in the Game   91

Chapter 8   Thirty-Something   115

Chapter 9   How to Stay Safe Doing Stand-Up   135

Chapter 10 Becoming Irene   155

Chapter 11 Me, Myself and Irene   173

Chapter 12 The Murky Depths   185

Chapter 13 Thank You, St Jude (and Coral)   197

Chapter 14 A Reason and a Lifetime   213

Chapter 15 Hatches, Matches and Dispatches   223

Chapter 16 Unapologetically Me   241

Acknowledgements   253

Foreword

If you picked up this book and just realised that my name is actually Lynne McGranger, *not* Irene Roberts, you're not alone. Happy to answer to both 'Lynne' and 'Irene' (but honestly, I prefer Lynne), you may know me from the diner in *Home and Away*'s fictitious Summer Bay. Or perhaps I taught your son tae kwan do, or was the receptionist at the chiropractor's, or worked at the butchers in Tenterfield … all things I've been accused of. Perhaps you've just seen my mug as you flicked through the channels on the telly.

As a self-confessed accident looking for a place to happen, I've recently taken time to look back on my life to try to make sense of how I've managed to 'play pretends' professionally for over forty years. If you'd asked me at eighteen if I'd ever be the longest-running female cast member on one of Australia's most successful soap operas, I would have laughed a cloud of marijuana smoke in your face. (Shocking, I know.)

And yet, here I am: twenty-nine years deep into *Home and Away*.

From a very young age, I could lie like a chop in gravy. It's not that I was malicious or conniving, I just found that it was an effective way of getting people to feel a certain way about me. It didn't matter if I was passing blame off on one of my friends or leading someone to believe I was a French backpacker, I loved the thrill of crafting a story.

It wasn't until I started teachers' college that I made the connection that lying is a lot like acting.

After joining the drama club and getting my feet wet, so to speak, I also realised that when you're acting, you get the chance to be all of the things society doesn't want you to be. In my twenties and thirties, I was very much a people-pleaser, which is why it was so invigorating to play the mean drunk, the sensual stripper, the sexist 1950s singer, or the meek wife who finally stands up to her domineering husband. When I momentarily gravitated towards comedy, I got to further indulge in the type of self-deprecating humour that borders on catharsis. I finally felt comfortable in my skin, both on- and offstage.

As you read about my personal and professional decisions in the following pages, it'll quickly become obvious that I'm not a 'life planner'. I didn't grow up with big dreams of being on TV or attending NIDA. I didn't map out a path to an awards podium.

The truth is, I'm more of a one-day-at-a-time kind of girl.

In an industry known for its turbulence and quest for the next big thing, I bet you're wondering how someone like me ends up getting to play the same character for nearly three decades. (I also bet you're wondering if I still smoke pot.) To understand that (and to answer your question), we need to go back to Sydney in 1955.

CHAPTER 1

A (Soap) Star is Born

If there's one universal truth to being a two-year-old, it's that *everything* looks big. For me, the Queens Park Tennis Courts chain-link fencing was the biggest. Every week, my parents Bruce and Audrey would play tennis there and I'd wander around nearby in my favourite chequered dress. Actually, it's quite possible this was my only dress because my mother sewed like she cooked; everything was kind of inedible and mostly unwearable. In those days, Dad was a struggling accountant, Mum was at home with me and the fact that she managed to sew a decent looking merry-go-round border at the bottom of this dress was truly the stuff of miracles.

Anyway, back in 1955 I was peering through one of the diamond-shaped openings in the fence desperate to see my parents. From birth, I'd been fiercely independent. I loved looking for bugs in the bushes, saying hello to families strolling by and every now and then catching my dad ace a point with his signature serve.

But there I was, sobbing; the definition of a terrified two-year-old.

I couldn't find them.

Convinced I was lost, my young mind began to spiral out of . control. Would I starve to death because I'd no longer be able to eat Mum's famous homemade Carnation milk ice cream? (One of the few edible things she ever made.) Would I have to sleep outside for the rest of my life?

As I feverishly imagined what my pretty chequered dress and blonde hair would look like covered in dirt, twigs and leaves, I heard my name being called.

'Lynne! Lynne! We're over here!'

To say that I was relieved to hear my parents' voices is an understatement. The endorphins that rushed through my body catapulted me from the fence and into my mum's arms. Turns out that the entire time I thought I was lost (which could have been either three minutes or three hours), I was actually in their sight.

You're probably thinking that age two is a bit young to hold such a clear memory, but I believe that you remember life's extreme highs and extreme lows, and the fear of being lost was an all-consuming low. Childhood trauma aside, I often think of the Queens Park Tennis Courts because in hindsight the experience foreshadowed a couple of common themes in my life:

1. Bugger. I'm lost. Again.
2. Why wait to see what happens when it's so much easier to panic now.

For nearly sixty years, I spent a lot of time feeling unsure. If someone asked, 'Who has two thumbs and over-thinks things?' I'd be the first person to shout, 'Me! Me!' From family to friendships to food to finding my mark on the first day of filming *Home and Away*, I've often felt unsettled and essentially 'lost'. Not 'who am I and what's the meaning of life?' lost, more 'all over the place like a mad woman's breakfast' lost.

But over the past decade or so, I've come to realise that I was probably no more lost than anyone else. Don't get me wrong – I can get *extremely* lost in a department store. If I don't take note of where I went in or what I went past, I can wander around DJs for days. (DJs Castle Hill knows to leave out food and water for me.) While not everyone may believe in the Sky Boss, I like to think that God had me everywhere I was supposed to be and with everyone I was supposed to be with. And that, of course, started with my mum and dad.

Growing up in post-World War II Australia meant having parents who wholeheartedly embraced 'keep calm and carry on' mentalities. While I knew Dad was on the first boat that made it to Changi after the Japanese surrendered and that he could barely form words about the trauma of seeing people dying of starvation, the only physical evidence of him being in the war was an old Samurai sword that he kept in the garage. For someone who was so scarred by his time in Singapore, why and how he chose to bring such a large (and possibly illegal) memento home still baffles me.

Mum meanwhile kept her trauma buried beneath a cloak of 1950s social norms. Prior to having me, she gave birth prematurely to my brother, Stewart, who only lived a few days. Aside from organising his burial, there were no acknowledgments of anniversaries, no visits to the cemetery, no counselling as far as I know … I'm not even sure when I found out about Stewart's brief life.

This was common for the era – two newlyweds bottling up their feelings and getting on with their lives – because that's just what you did, right? That said, I do not recall Dad bottling *any* of his emotions when it came to being sick, which was seemingly all the time. He had a weak chest from smoking like a chimney, as well as terrible ears from spending years during the war wearing headphones and listening for submarines. As a result, he regularly hopscotched between bronchitis and middle ear infections. Mum on the other hand had an immune system as strong as a Mallee bull. Unfortunately, this made her a very apathetic caregiver.

As someone who could talk under wet cement pretty much from birth, I like to think I was a nice distraction for my parents and the baggage they brought to our family unit. Often described as 'gregarious' and fully aware that I wasn't 'good with my own company', I simply wanted to be near people, especially other kids. I remember being fascinated by the children who'd walk past our house to and from school every morning. Desperate to emulate them, I'd role-play with my satchel that I needed to catch the bus. When it would fly by, I'd yell, 'Missed the damn thing!' (Much to my mother's amusement.)

Ironically, when my sister, Paula, came along when I was four, I couldn't have been *less* enthused. (Sorry, Paula, you know I love you ... now.) I don't know if I was too young to be maternal, too old to relate or simply too self-absorbed to pay anyone with my shared DNA attention, but I considered her a bad smell that wouldn't stop following me around. As far as I could see, Paula had nothing to offer. She couldn't make me snacks, she didn't have toys that I didn't have and she definitely couldn't provide the type of audience participation I deemed acceptable when I was performing in the living room.

Regardless of my lack of excitement about having a sibling, I absolutely loved home life and always felt safe. Dad got an accounting job for Coles (the department store, not the supermarket) while Mum continued to stay home to look after us kids. When I was about five, Coles asked us to house swap with another employee's family in Melbourne for a year. Enthusiastic about our interstate adventure and curious about all the new kids I'd get to meet, I was relieved to hear that we'd be flying south instead of driving. For much of my childhood, I got horribly carsick. I will never forget Dad driving us in his grey and white FC Holden up the NSW coast on the old Pacific Highway every Easter and Christmas holidays. This was pre-freeway and pre-air conditioning, which meant one lane of winding road and temperatures that turned our red vinyl car seats into the equivalent of a metal slippery dip in the outback. Even though I was looking forward to the flight to Melbourne, I have no recollection of it. I don't know if it was just because I was five and living in my own La La Land or if my parents drugged me because I was such a pain in the arse. What I do remember is blinking my eyes and 'nek minit' we were in Heidelberg.

While many who moved to Victoria in the late 1950s were excited about exploring the nearby limestone coastline, spotting a penguin on Phillip Island or seeing Australia's tallest building at the time in person (ICI House), I was excited about making new friends.

Paula was still very much a baby, so Mum was busy washing (and defrosting) cloth nappies. No matter how much we mentally prepared for the cold Melbourne weather, Mum often forgot about the freezing temperatures and would peg the nappies out to dry in the evening. The next day, it looked like she was collecting pizza boxes off the line.

Dad was enjoying his job and had also taken a keen interest in making his own ginger beer. This was all well and good until that same cold weather caused his freshly bottled brews to freeze and explode under the house. Convinced World War III was about to break out, I jumped out of bed in a panic before reminding myself that it was Dad's booze – not bazookas – making all the racket.

With my parents preoccupied with babies and carbonated beverages, I spent my days walking to and from school with the neighbourhood kids before luring them home to watch *Circus Boy* with Mickey Dolenz, *Rin Tin Tin*, *Hopalong Cassidy* and *Casey Jones*. As the first family on the street with a TV, you better believe I quickly became popular.

While those kids may have just been there to ogle the whopping fifteen-inch screen in our lounge room, I also like to think they appreciated my budding domestic skills. As they'd lie on their bellies glued to the tube, I'd go into the kitchen and prepare afternoon tea. Clearly taking after my mother, this little 'Lynne Special' usually involved me carefully slicing Arnott's Orange Slice biscuits into halves and pouring out equal servings of matching orange cordial. (The green cordial was for posh people.) Once our shows ended and our stomachs were full of what now might be considered toxic chemicals (no offence, Arnott's), we'd be back on the street in search of locust shells to collect and onion grass to munch on.

On a scale of one to ten with one representing 'being born fully clothed' and ten representing 'resident of a nudist colony', my mum's modesty was somewhere between a one and a two. Many mornings, I'd watch in awe as she changed into her clothing for the day without taking off her nightie first, which was as mystifying as David Copperfield making the Harbour Bridge disappear. Curious to see if I'd inherited my mother's powers, I attempted to put my school uniform on before taking off my nightie. While I definitely looked a lot less graceful than my mum, I did it! With only seconds until my friends would arrive to walk to school, I dashed out the door feeling chuffed that I had yet another party trick to add to my repertoire of talents.

Roughly ten steps down the footpath, though, I realised I had forgotten one very important aspect of the magic trick. My knickers! Nothing lets you know you're bare-bottomed like a 'hello!' from a gust of Melbourne wind under a school uniform. Luckily, the kids were happy to wait for me while I ran back inside to grab my underwear.

A lot of my memories from this time do not include my parents. It's probably because most people didn't have cars and if they did, the men needed them to get to work. If a mother had a baby to take care of then the bigger kids simply walked to and from school alone. At least that's how it was for me. I know I sound like an old geezer saying this, but *in my day* I used to walk fifteen miles ... barefoot ... in the snow ... on my knees! (Luxury! – for my fellow *Monty Python* fans.) But it's nearly true – my five-year-old legs tore up the streets of Heidelberg day in day out. It's a shame I wasn't walking for a cause because I would have scored some major sponsorship money for the distances I logged. In those days, there was an innocence that meant kids ran freely between home, school, friends' houses and the shops.

But then a series of awful events ensured little hands were held tighter, doors were locked longer and children everywhere felt a fear that would forever change the way they looked at strangers.

In Sydney in 1960, eight-year-old Graeme Thorne was kidnapped and murdered. While I was never told this directly, I overheard my parents talking about it. By 1965 we would hear about the Wanda Beach murders, and a year later the disappearance of the Beaumont children in Adelaide. In a world where true crime didn't have its own TV, podcast and film genres, it was confronting trying to digest this news – especially as a child.

Years later, I found out my maternal grandmother was the chief witness for the prosecution in the murder of Linda Agostini aka the 'Pyjama Girl'. I started believing that murder was a real possibility for me, which is why I adopted a more cautious approach. And by 'cautious approach' I mean that I was still oblivious to my surroundings, inherently naive and definitely too trusting.

Mum made me carry a hatpin wherever I went.

When it came time to bid Heidelberg farewell and move back to our home in Miranda in Sydney's south, I started a new school all over again. Armed with a youthful energy that means you never tire of introductions and small talk, I couldn't wait to tell everyone about my interstate adventures. I'll never forget sitting in class and the maths teacher quizzing us on how many months were in a year. I confidently wrote *thirteen*. This was because I distinctly recalled Mum telling me that we were going to Melbourne 'for a year' *but* I had also overheard her tell someone that we were there for 'thirteen months'.

Because I was a child genius, I put two and two together and got five.

Apparently, I was wrong and had a full-on barney with the teacher about it. Turns out Mum was just generally ball-parking in a roundabout sort of way. The good news is becoming a mathematician wasn't something I cared about.

Nope, I only had eyes for friends, food and show tunes.

Lucky for me, my parents had a turntable and an impressive collection of LPs. When I wasn't watching them sing along to Dick Powell and the Mills Brothers, I'd spend hours singing and dancing to the soundtracks of *My Fair Lady*, *Can-Can*, *Gigi*, *Guys and Dolls*, *Oklahoma!*, *West Side Story*, and of course, *South Pacific*. I knew every line of *My Fair Lady*, even the male parts.

Once I grew confident in my abilities, I began soliciting donations from my parents' friends to watch me perform in our backyard. While they were probably more focused on the alcoholic drinks on offer, I remember them being a very engaging audience with lots of threepences to spare! This had a big impact on where I eventually ended up in life. Had I had a better voice, I would have loved to have done professional musical theatre. As it turns out, I've got a bit of a gin voice. So unless I'm playing Jimmy Barnes or Tom Waits in a musical, any other role would require a vocal dexterity I just don't have.

These backyard performances happened nearly every night of the week in the school holidays. Even if I was exhausted after a night of show tunes, I'd still wake up bright-eyed and bushy-tailed for church every Sunday. As a practising Anglican, Dad made sure that Paula and I went to Sunday School. That meant freshly washed hair, a fluffy and very prickly green jumper, a grey woollen skirt and a pancake hat ringed with artificial flowers. Fetching, eh?

Throughout much of my childhood, I enjoyed the social side of church, but nothing the minister was saying really sank in. I guess this speaks volumes about my lack of connection with anything that didn't have to do with me.

Looking back, I now realise I only liked going to church for the following reasons:

1. I could covertly use my allocated collection plate money to go across the street to Donuts Galore and – you guessed it – eat donuts galore (as well as hot chips!).
2. When I was older, I'd get lots of attention by

participating in the Youth Group. Especially male attention …

3. The simple act of going made my parents proud of me. I was a self-confessed parent- and people-pleaser, so this was extremely important – even from a young age.

Reasons I *didn't* like going to church:

1. There was nothing about Lynne McGranger in the Bible.
2. The church did not endorse lying. (Nor embezzling the collection plate money for that matter.)

As someone who can lie like a rug, the church's opposing stance on the subject was not appreciated. It's funny, even though I was a people-pleaser, the six-year-old version of me was more than willing to break rules, be deceitful and keep secrets. It wasn't so much about doing the right thing, but more about making my parents *think* I was doing the right thing.

I remember hanging out with two particular girls, Christine and Anne. If three's a crowd when you're an adult, then three might as well be Circular Quay on New Year's Eve when you're a kid. (Way too much happening for someone not to leave in tears.) I didn't like Anne and she didn't like me, but we both liked Christine. This meant a lot of me willing myself to tolerate Anne.

One day I stood on our backyard sprinkler and broke it. When confronted with the evidence and a very disappointed look on my father's face, I shook my head and explained that it had been Anne who broke the sprinkler. The ease with which I bore false witness must have had some sort of karmic effect because the only other memory of Anne I have is when her mother chased me down the street with a broom, yelling, 'Good riddance to bad rubbish!'

I don't know what I did, but I'm sure it didn't warrant *that* sort of a response.

Luckily, our time in Miranda was coming to an end. I was destined for a fresh start ... in Brighton-Le-Sands.

CHAPTER 2
Eating for Australia

If strategically picking your friends based on the type of food they have at their house is wrong, I don't want to be right. As a child of parents who rationed the good biscuits and only served food that had been boiled to the point of no return, seeking out snacks was my most important extracurricular activity. Catholic families were always a solid choice because even though they seemed to have less money to go around due to the abundance of kids, they always had huge loaves of bread, scrumptiously sweet jams and my personal favourite: lashings of butter.

When we moved to Brighton-Le-Sands, the Catholics in the street were the Taylor family. I quickly became tight with their middle child of six (at last count), Gloria, who'd invite me round and fill my stomach with more carbs than an ultra-marathon runner would ever need. After my digestive tract was working at capacity, she'd let me look under the bed at their glow-in-the-dark nativity scenes and hold her mother's coveted gold statues of Jesus and Mary. I liked to pretend that I'd won an Oscar. Sadly, my daydreaming was always disrupted by shrill yips, barks and whines.

You see, the Taylors were as good at breeding puppies as they were kids.

But I clung to Gloria's friendship and grew to love the loud, fur-covered puppy mill they called their home. I did the same with Pam Stone, who lived a couple of streets away. Pam embraced the subtle art of not giving a f*ck from a very early age. Weirdly, I don't associate my friendship with her with food. No, when I think of Pam, I think of pee-laughing, partaking in what would now be considered bullying and of course roller skating. After fastening a rope around my waist and tying it to the frame of Pam's yellow Malvern Star, she'd take off down Barton Street. It was wildly exhilarating even if, bouncing along behind her on my backside, I looked more like a contestant on a Japanese game show than queen of the roller derby.

The real reason I think I clung to these friendships is because around the age of ten, Gloria, Pam and I became aware of our 'bottom dweller' status at school. Why? Well, Gloria had an unfortunate bowl cut and dogs so inbred they often came out with five legs and two heads, so this kind of made sense. And Pam didn't give two figs about trying to fit in, so I felt like her carefree attitude was the culprit.

But as for me, I couldn't work out why I wasn't 'in' with the cool kids. I knew I made people laugh (with me, not at me) and I could hold a deep discussion about the latest episode of *Sugarfoot*. (Confession: I actually never watched an episode, but that didn't stop me telling my peers detailed storylines. I don't know if I was magically guessing the storylines or if they were just nodding because they hadn't watched it either.)

Accolades and TV fortune telling aside, my first effort to elevate my social status involved something that required athleticism and a level of hand-eye coordination I wasn't sure I had: netball. Cheryl, Colleen and Kay aka the Scary Netball Girls (#SNBG) had been playing since kindergarten, which meant I had a lot of catching up to do. Equally passionate about the uniforms and the chance to eat oranges as I was about winning their friendship, I went down to Ramsgate Netball Park to try out. Not surprisingly, I made the B team and was told to play Wing Defence, which is the one spot you drop if you're short a player. This was completely fine with me because it turns out having a ball repeatedly slammed into my face and my fingers contorted out of recognition was something I loved about as much as clowns.

Seeing as my quest to become a Scary Netball Girl wasn't panning out, I had to think on my feet if I was going to get in with a cool clique. While I may not have shown any mental agility on the netball court, I was ingenious when it came to hatching plans. I came up with an idea: I'd join the Beatles Club. The club met at lunch to discuss lyrics, performances and of course which Beatle was the dreamiest. But instead of delivering the latest gossip from *Teen Life* magazine and wooing my classmates with my in-depth Ringo trivia, I spent most of the time trying to swap my Vita-Weats for white bread rolls loaded with egg, butter and lettuce. I know that this would be considered a COVID nightmare today, but back then, I was desperate for decent food.

I may have lacked the coordination for netball and occasionally confused Ringo with George, but boy, could I dance. During what I now refer to as the 'Dance Concert Incident of 1963', I owned the stage. Or so I thought. I was blissfully unaware that

I actually resembled one of the hippos from *Fantasia*. Mum was in the audience and the woman beside her gave her an earful.

'Gee, that girl's a good dancer. It's a shame she's so *big*.'

I don't know what was more upsetting: that this woman voiced her opinion or that Mum proceeded to tell me all about it. From that point on, she liked to remind me that I would 'get fat' every time I opened my mouth to take a bite of something and made it her mission to get me trim.

It was the 1960s and society had no issue with Mum putting her young daughter on a series of fad diets ... supplemented by a range of appetite suppressants and laxatives. First there was the Banana and Milk Diet. For some reason I also recall eating ham on this diet, but that could have been me cheating ... Next came the Grapefruit Diet. After that it was the Oranges, Tuna and Milk Diet. I once made the horrific mistake of eating these out of sequence. Everything curdled in my stomach, immediately came back up and as a result, I couldn't look at those three things for years.

Even though Mum's efforts to help me shed some kilograms might be considered extreme (but apparently came from a place of love), she did let me buy lunch from the school canteen on Thursdays. This was meat pie day and being able to peel off the lid and squirt sauce into that hot gristly mush was nearly as good as Christmas morning.

After all this dietary intervention, you're probably imagining young Lynne wasting away and living off of crumbs blowing in the wind down the school halls … but here's the thing: I was about as good at sticking to a diet as I am at sticking to the point. I ate the weird food Mum provided *plus* everyone else's food from the canteen, which was bizarrely called the Oslo. I'm guessing in deference to the capital of Norway whose citizens I can only assume were seen as the pinnacle of fit and trim humanity.

But eating three slices of bread and butter with cheese, ham, peanut butter with fruit *and* my Vita-Weats and Vegemite (otherwise known as worm biscuits) *and* Phillipa Bridger's fabulous egg, lettuce and mayonnaise sandwiches, it's no wonder I tipped the scales at close to eighty kilograms by the time I turned fourteen. While I know the Australian school system meant well by introducing that Scandinavian meal plan, who on earth can stay slim on three slices of bread, butter, cheese, fruit, veg and raw cabbage? (Apparently everyone but me …)

Accustomed to bending so far backwards trying to fit in with my peers that I could have been part of the Flying Fruit Fly Circus, getting Mr Sinclair as a teacher in Year 5 couldn't have come at a better time. On top of wild antics like delivering lessons while simultaneously pacing the room and thumping a staff, jumping in and out of windows, biting chalk and throwing it at you, and teaching us how to decipher hieroglyphics, he also found an effective way to make me genuinely interested in English Royal history, Egyptology, maths and even chess. None of these things really had anything to do with either food or me, so my attention was quite unexpected.

This was a pivotal year because it was the first time someone to whom I wasn't related and whom I truly respected made me feel smart, talented, heard and accepted. I instinctively knew that Mr Sinclair approved of me and that approval made me try harder.

I even came first in the class that year ... for the girls. It was a bone of contention between me and Roger Wilson, whom Pam and I called 'Busy' because he was such a busybody. He was also the first asthmatic I ever met.

Another confession: one time we pushed Busy over and he had a full-on asthma attack that required medical attention. I couldn't believe it at the time, but he didn't dob on us. (Told you we were bullies. #notproud) That's why even though he beat me by half a mark on a geography project which made him first in the class, I let it slide. Okay fine, I let it slide because I took umbrage and tried to convince Mr Sinclair that I had outperformed Busy in maths and we should *at least* be tied for first.

That got a hard no from Mr Sinclair.

Since I felt both terror and admiration for him, I accepted his ruling. Even though he would cane us across the hands for passing notes in class, he was such a good teacher and by far my favourite. I mean, when you compare him to Mr O'Brien, who smoked cigarettes in the playground, and Ms Howard, who vacillated between making us capture and tag butterflies to delivering whacks across the back of our legs just-because, it wasn't tough competition.

The 1960s were wild, eh? Teachers belting kids, cigarette smoke blanketing the playground and, lest we forget, the news that stopped the world. Just like the news of Princess Diana dying, I will never forget where I was when I heard JFK had been shot. It was Saturday morning in Australia (Friday in Texas for the sticklers) and I had just saddled up at the kitchen table to eat my boiled egg, which Mum had murdered, and toast soldiers soaked in margarine. I'd tied an apron around my neck as a makeshift, oversized bib. My parents must have been pottering about outside because when the news came on the radio, my gasp was the only one audible in the house. I immediately put down my spoon and hopped off the chair.

When I found Mum and Dad and told them about the tragedy, they did not believe me. 'Don't be ridiculous, Lynne!' my mother said with a chuckle. I'm pretty sure Dad even told me to stop making stuff up. While I admit that taking anything seriously from a ten-year-old wearing a bib is difficult, I was miffed that they were questioning my integrity. I was also distraught because this was the first time someone I deemed invincible, eternal and untouchable had died. While I know JFK wasn't family, he was a fixture on our TV along with the beautiful Jackie. Together they made me feel that no matter what happened at school or on my street, I'd still have their wise words, stunning wardrobe choices and warm smiles to comfort me.

Suddenly, life felt fragile. If someone like JFK could be shot, what might happen to me? A few years earlier, a neighbour's two-year-old daughter died of leukemia. As a seven-year-old, I don't recall being afraid of death or that my own life was threatened in any way by this news. But I was aware of her parents' intense sadness and felt really sorry for them. Now three years older and perhaps wiser, I knew that it didn't matter if you were a king or a pauper – every day could be your last.

As clichéd as it may sound, the news of JFK's assassination changed the way I spent time with my family. When I wasn't at school or tearing up the streets (and my bum) on roller skates, I loved going fishing with Dad and my grandfather, whom we called Pa. Our go-to spot was Botany Bay, which is where I caught my first fish. It was a whiting and even though I think the fish actually decided to end its own life that day, I was exceptionally proud.

Getting to spend time with Pa meant the world to me. My grandparents lived in one of those liver brick flats in Bondi, which made school holidays extra fun. Pa was a shift worker so he'd take me down to the beach in the morning where he'd rescue me from getting dumped by huge waves and then cheer me on as I squashed washed-up bluebottles with my bare feet. Nana would make me tomato on toast with salt and pepper, which was much appreciated after having endured my mother's meal plan every school term. In the arvos, Pa would have a nap, so Nana would take me to the shops or to swim at Pa's sister's house in Rose Bay.

I thought my great-aunt Florence was posh because she had a swimming pool and a grandfather clock. Turns out she was posh because she was married to the former Lord Mayor of Sydney, Reginald Bartley. Here's something for your next Lynne McGranger Trivia Night: the Kings Cross library was named after great-aunt Florence and the Rushcutters Bay oval after great-uncle Reginald!

At night, Nana would heat up fish fingers and potato crisps in the oven. I'm not joking – she literally laid potato crisps on a baking tray and popped them in the oven. I think this was supposed to be the vegetable component of the meal, which explains in part why they were always rolling me around. After dinner, we'd have a very small bowl of Cadbury chocolate squares. Even though I come from a long line of people who can't cook, I always left feeling full and loved.

Don't get me wrong, I still felt plenty of love at home from Bruce and Audrey. Even my sister Paula was less of an annoyance by now. It's just my inability to stop eating was becoming a common topic of conversation. Perhaps Mum saw something in me she recognised in herself. After a couple of years of failing diet after diet, I decided to try something I'd seen Dad doing: swallowing Ford Pills. Laxatives. I didn't want to forgo binging on two shillings' worth of devon with Diane Hemphill, so I thought I could just balance my intake by revving up my output …

And that, my friends, is how you develop an eating disorder.

CHAPTER 3
Are You There, God? It's Me, Lynne

Like many eleven-year-old girls, I longed for three things:

1. Attention from boys
2. Boobs
3. My period

Annoyingly, the third thing on my list came before the other two. While Mum had given me the obligatory book to read about what was happening to my body, I definitely didn't absorb (no pun intended) much about the menstruating part. Okay, that's not true, I recall recognising the tell-tale brownish stain in my undies after a day of fishing in a tinny with Dad. It was 25 January 1965 ... oddly, my sister's birthday. Equal parts excited and concerned, I dug out the stash of pads Mum had strategically placed into my dresser drawer months before.

Well, I waited and waited and waited but my period didn't come until Anzac Day. As Australia played two-up and paid respect to our fallen diggers, I proudly rubbed my crampy belly and basked in the glory of knowing that I was officially a woman fit for boobs, boys and business. To this day I can't eat an Anzac biscuit without getting nostalgic.

I don't know if I was feeling empowered by the lining of my uterus exiting my body or what, but I decided to take item number two on my list into my own hands. Boobs. You see, Mum had discreetly slipped two second-hand bras into my dresser drawer. Since they didn't have any padding, I experimented with wadding up toilet paper and folding socks to form the perfect B cup. The toilet paper was more realistic, in case you were wondering.

As I'd strut up and down the street with no other purpose than showing off my new rack, I grew increasingly giddy at the thought of people noticing. Unfortunately the only attention I got was from Robert, who lived two streets away. Robert was cute, but it was obvious that he was into me and let's be honest – even the most mature women tend to want what they cannot have. Robert's affection made me so awkward that watching movies over the school holidays at his house felt more like a stint in detention than a youthful elbow-knocking date that ends in sweaty hand-holding.

Never mind. Next up was Ricky. We used to ride bikes together, which was great until he started flying airplane love letters into my yard. When Dad found one asking me to meet Ricky at Courtney's Corner, the same awkward feeling washed over me and I wanted to crawl under a rock. Given the fact I was literally praying for male attention at church, I was genuinely confused by how uncomfortable it made me feel.

That is until two years later when Owen came into the picture.

Owen was the type of dreamy fella you write about in your diary. Obviously one's words and musings are so heated and filled with passion, they're *nothing* your parents should ever lay eyes on. Yes, this type of love must be writ in code.

Dear Diary,
eht yaw newo nniuq skool ta em sekam ym traeh dnuop. Di od
gnihtyna ot leef sih spil no enim.
I evol uoy reverof, newo
ennyl

While I thought my code-writing abilities were worthy of a James Bond novel, my mother had no trouble deciphering the entries, which made making eye contact with her rather uncomfortable for the summer of 1966.

Sadly, my love for Owen was unrequited. When people say the boys they liked never noticed them, they probably mean while walking down a hallway or in a classroom. When I say Owen didn't notice me, I mean I have literally been on a boat with him and two others and he would have only looked for three life jackets if we were going down.

Word on the street was that he liked Christine. The perfect combination of pretty, skinny and cool, Christine's presence amplified the fact that my body more closely resembled Gru from *Minions* than an eleven-year-old girl. I seriously looked like a candy apple teetering on a wooden stick. This first crush rejection stung like seawater in a cut and lingered long until I found out the reason Owen didn't notice me. Turns out he was dancing at the other end of the ballroom!

Suddenly the rejection didn't feel so personal.

Even though it was Owen's sexuality that made him not like me, it wouldn't hurt to have had more of a physique like Christine's. When my school friends decided to do the annual 40-Hour Famine in Year 9 (which I had failed one hour into in previous years), I figured this was a good way to lose some weight. The Ford Pills had been helping me feel less guilty about scoffing food my mother didn't approve of, but sadly I just wasn't shedding those pounds.

Just as dismayed at the results, Mum took me to the doctor's where I was prescribed Tenuate Dospan and thyroxine. Unless you're a truck driver, a pharmacist or dabbling in diet pills, you may not know that Tenuate Dospan is essentially speed. This is mind-blowing now because from the time I could walk, I needed speed like a fish needs a bicycle. To this day, I'm always an eleven out of ten. Thyroxine, on the other hand, was simply a synthetic version of the hormone needed to keep your thyroid in working order. A very odd thing to be put on as a child. The good news is: I lost weight! The bad news: it all came back ... and then some.

Even though society (and Mum) may not have loved my body, I was rather indifferent and still more than happy to find ways to eat a few – okay, *a lot* – of my favourite things. A golden opportunity came when Mum had a hysterectomy. She had to spend a week in hospital, which meant I got to apply what little I retained from Miss Rapmund in home economics and make crumbed cutlets for Dad, Paula and me. As the fat for the crumbed cutlets heats up, you use little squares of bread to determine if the fat is hot enough. Turns out these are delicious. Turns out I may have discovered a culinary secret: croutons!

Long story short: I still enjoy crumbed cutlets and croutons to this day.

While I continued to take *all* the pills and eat the Vita-Weats Mum dished out for me instead of the juicy burgers and chips the rest of my family would enjoy on Sundays, I was a happy and confident teen. I didn't spend much time checking myself out in front of a full-length mirror. I was too busy hanging out with friends like Jill. Together we'd spend hours choreographing dances to 'Wouldn't It Be Nice' in her bedroom. When we needed a break, we'd watch episodes of *Kommotion* for inspiration.

The only downside of hanging out with Jill was having to witness her parents' loveless marriage. I found it childish how they'd ignore each other. I had never seen a grown man treat his wife like she was an annoying breeze blowing through the room. I'd also never seen a glare that figuratively slapped a man across the face. When the passive-aggressive vibes reached a level of nine or ten, Jill and I were out the door.

More often than not, we'd find our way to the beach and gossip about our crushes and which celebrity danced the best on *Kommotion*. I always thought Denise Drysdale was the most talented. Boy could that girl go-go. One afternoon while wandering home, a couple of boys on a balcony yelled out, 'Hey, dreamboat!' Admittedly flattered to be getting cat-called, when I looked up to bat my eyelashes as if to ask, 'Who, me?', they burst into laughter and shouted, 'Not *you*, shipwreck!' While both Jill and I found this absolutely hilarious, it was one of the first times I learnt that I needed to rely on my personality.

Luckily for me, a lot of people seemed to appreciate my humour, which made attending Youth Group on a Friday night borderline enjoyable. Actually, it was really enjoyable. Yes, it was something Dad always had to twist my arm to do, but I liked the kids who went and felt proud when I got an answer right during Bible trivia (or got to play spin the bottle).

As a Christian kid who mostly just prayed if I was in a pickle or wanted Owen Quinn to like me, I wasn't that thrilled about attending a scheduled Billy Graham concert with my Youth Group, but when I got there I was surprisingly moved. I don't know if it was Billy's southern accent, which reminded me of Atticus Finch, or the tens of thousands of evangelical voices singing praises, but I left feeling inspired to be a good Christian and make good choices.

But then I met Margaret, who introduced me to her brother and his friends.

These guys were full-on rev heads with lead feet and souped-up Holdens and Wolseleys. At the time I was still going to Youth Group and listening to Simon and Garfunkel's entire *Parsley, Sage, Rosemary and Thyme* album alone in my bedroom, so as you can imagine, I was infatuated with these boys and their wild ways. It didn't matter if we were double shuffling through the S-bends, street racing, or committing to memory every Holden up until and including 1968, I was in heaven. I can still rattle them off today, year and model, in case you wondered.

Of course, I had a major crush on one member of the group: Andrew Reinhardt.

My family had moved to Carrs Park by this stage so I would walk the four kilometres down through the bush, around the road and then past the park to meet up with Margaret, her brothers and in particular, Andrew. As always, Mum would make me carry a hatpin for protection. While everyone was busy listening to music and playing cards, I was trying to win Andrew's attention. Aside from offering me a ride home one evening, he didn't like me *like that*, but evidently Jill's boyfriend's friend, Dennis, did.

Dennis began studying engineering but left uni to become a cop so he could ride around on motorbikes. Ironically, he hung out with (what I now refer to as) the Ermington Mob. It was odd that he was mates with these bad boys because they were legitimate small-time crims. They used to do stuff like drive through Kings Cross and egg people. (I may also be guilty of this ...)

What I'm *not* guilty of – I swear I was just a witness – was the time a guy called Weasel, who was in and out of juvie on a regular basis, stole a front-end loader and drove it through the streets of Guildford. Weasel managed to knock over a few phone boxes before allowing the huge machine to topple into a quarry. Thankfully, he leapt to safety seconds before it went over the edge.

Nothing like this *ever* happened in Youth Group.

I'd like to say that was the last time I got myself into a questionable situation, but the truth is, there are thirteen chapters left in this book. I loved the sense of danger that came with hanging out with Margaret's brother and his mates. Not that my life had been terribly vanilla in any sense, but there was something about breaking the rules that excited me.

What didn't excite me was Dennis.

Yet again, it was a case of a boy liking me more than I liked him. I knew it was over when I'd arrive home from school and find him sitting in our kitchen chatting with my mum (who thought he was the cat's pyjamas). I'd pretty much just ignore him. #meangirls

After breaking up with Dennis, I decided to return my focus to school. At this point I was attending Moorefield Girls' High in Kogarah. Mum volunteered in the canteen, which was convenient because I'd put about twenty cents in the till and then take $2 worth of food. (This might be up there with stealing the collection plate money.) Armed with ample snacks, I approached a girl named Debbie. Both equally passionate about food, boys and wagging school, we hit it off instantly. Together, we made attending first class roll call and then skiving off the rest of the day our modus operandi.

When the weather was warm, we'd go down to the beach and pretend to be French foreign exchange students. I was Pascale and Debbie was Annick. While our act usually only went as far as some witty banter in a bad French accent, one day our charade escalated when a guy named Robert seemed to fall head over heels in love with me. And by me I mean Pascale. I ended up giving him 'her' number. To my horror, he phoned soon after to ask Pascale out. The only issue was her cousin 'Lynne' had to answer the phone ... In a manner similar to Robin Williams in *Mrs Doubtfire*, I'd swap voices as I called out for Pascale.

'Paaaaascale,' I'd shout in my best ocker accent.

'Oui, Lynne,' I'd respond in a carefree, breathless, don't-shave-my-armpits, escargot-munching voice.

'Robbo's on the phone for ya.'

'Merci! Roberrrrrt, is so good to 'ear from you.'

This type of exchange went on for about three weeks. Finally, it got to be too much so I decided to end it. This may have been the earliest form of 'newsjacking' but around this time President de Gaulle died. Boom. I had a plan.

Ring ring ...

'Paaaaascale! Robbo's on the phone again.'

Cue: tears.

'Roberrrrrrt, I have such sad news. I must go back to Paris tomorrow for President de Gaulle's funeral. I am so sorry, but I don't think we can talk anymore.'

Yes, Robert was sad.

Yes, it was wrong that I lied.

But also yes, I was a *genius* for using President de Gaulle's death as an excuse!

This may very well have been one of the first times I thought to myself that I was a pretty good actor.

Some people might say it's bullshit, but I'm impressed with my ability to craft a character, get an audience member emotionally invested and end the story with a bang. The only downside was that Debbie and I had to stop going to the beach for fear of running into Robert. Luckily it was getting close to winter. Even luckier: Debbie started dating a guy named Gil, who, I would be happy to learn, had a friend named John.

CHAPTER 4
Seventeen Going on Ten

I'm not sure if there's an official copy of the Girl Code, but I am sure that somewhere in there it says: if your friend needs you to be a wingwoman, you put on your most flattering (but not *too* flattering) flight suit and take to the open skies. And that's exactly what I was doing for Debbie one sunny day in 1970. Except instead of being in a fighter jet, we were heading over to Gil's house so that Debbie could get her flirt on. Little did I know, we were about to walk into a front lawn carwash scene straight out of a teenage romcom.

That's right – Gil and another guy were both shirtless, sudsy and totally aware that their matching six-packs were reflecting off the bonnet of a white Valiant. While Gil grabbed some Tabs for us, I found out his friend was named John David Leslie Gilmour and that he was currently living in a caravan out the back. Twenty-four to my seventeen, I was fascinated by what I perceived as John's vagabond lifestyle, cheeky grin and exceptionally strong jawline. (To this day, I can't see a bus advertisement of Fitzy from Fitzy and Wippa without thinking of him.) Did I mention his six-pack, too? Even better, John had just broken up with his long-time girlfriend. She lived with her family directly across the street from him. Needing to put literal and figurative distance between them, he decided to set up in Gil's backyard.

When you're seventeen and finally receiving male attention from a man you find shockingly handsome, funny and just the right amount of dangerous, it's easy to fall in love. I'm talking appetite-suppressing, all-consuming, to-the-moon-and-back *love*. (Okay, let's be honest – not even my prescribed speed was suppressing my appetite at this point. John's nickname for me was Spud.)

I was in Year 12 at the time while John worked as a truck driver. Each morning I'd wake up early and go sit by our kitchen window, high up on a hill with a perfect view of the Princes Highway. I'd then patiently wait to see John flash his truck headlights at me as he drove by. That quick flickering of lights always made my heart skip a beat. It also made staying focused at school impossible. Instead of studying for the HSC or paying any sort of attention to my assignments, I'd doodle 'Mrs John Gilmour' on my notebook or ditch school entirely to join John on his drives.

One weekend, I told my parents I was staying at Debbie's, but really John and I drove up to Port Stephens. We ate fish and chips on the beach, went for long walks and had the types of deep and meaningful talks that start in the afternoon and go until 2 a.m. the next day. It only took a few short months of us dating for me to decide that John was the one – the person I wanted to go all the way with, which happened soon after at his place.

Yes, my cherry was popped in a caravan in a suburban backyard.

Here's the thing about having sex at seventeen in the 1970s: unless you came from a family that openly discussed it and wouldn't have judged if you wanted to have pre-marital relations, it was kind of hard to know about contraception. What's *not* hard to know is that a skipped period usually only means one of two things: you're stressed or you're pregnant.

In my case, it was the latter. (Followed by the former.)

I'm not sure if the trauma of my teen pregnancy caused some unintentional memory loss, but I really can't remember experiencing any major pregnancy symptoms. I also don't remember how I told John. What I do remember is that he was incredibly loving and made me feel safe. Knowing that my parents would be horrified to find out that on top of me recently failing the HSC (damn doodling), my budding relationship had already resulted in a pregnancy, I started hatching a plan. John mentioned moving to Perth so that he could get a better job. He may have just said this as a flippant idea, but my seventeen-year-old brain clung to the thought and immediately began envisioning driving across the country hand in hand.

When we got to the west coast, we'd get married straight away and then stay in a caravan park until we could find a flat to rent. While John worked, I'd get second-hand baby items from the Salvos and put the nursery together. Once I was set up, I'd call my parents and tell them our news and that I had everything sorted. Of course, they wouldn't be as mad that I was pregnant because they'd see how responsible and capable I was.

Yep, I had it all figured out.

With my mind busy mentally preparing for our future together, I was caught off guard when I came home from school one day. Instead of being at work or doing jobs around the house, my parents were sitting in the lounge room, evidently waiting for me. The look on Dad's face and the tears in Mum's eyes told me immediately that the jig was up. There were no excuses, and no escape. I sat down and braced myself.

'John called and told us that you're pregnant,' Dad said.

Oh, did he ... I thought to myself. I looked down and nodded. 'Yes.'

What followed next was my dad's pragmatic response to a heartbreaking predicament: I'd have to terminate my pregnancy and get a job. While this was definitely *not* part of my 'run away to Perth' plan, I was relieved that I didn't have to keep such a big secret anymore. And deep down I knew that John calling my parents behind my back was a testament to his integrity. He was worried about my future.

I looked up and couldn't handle seeing Mum's tear-stained cheeks. This woman *never* cried. At that moment, I simply wanted to do whatever they said, even if it meant having an abortion.

On 18 January 1971, Mum took me to a nondescript building in Kings Cross. We went through two thick and heavy metal doors and entered a room that wasn't in a hospital or medical centre, but still felt very clinical. Abortions were illegal in those days, so I don't know how Mum was even able to make the appointment. I imagined those big, heavy doors were to prevent anyone from entering without permission. What I do know is that the doctor and nurse were very sympathetic and non-judgmental and before I knew it, I was back in the car with Mum and we were on our way home.

While some might feel cheated having their choice essentially taken away, I was not mature enough or mentally equipped to even comprehend the repercussions of deciding to keep a baby. My obsession with making my parents proud and preserving my love for John overrode the fact that I had aborted a foetus, which shows just how very much of a child I was myself.

Ultimately, I just wanted everything to go back to the way it was: *normal*.

As my brain finished developing and I eventually grew into the person I am proud to be today, my abortion is not something I've lived with lightly. I have moments of regret and countless moments of 'what if?'. Over the past fifty years, I've found myself asking things like: if I had kept my baby, would I still have found my love for acting? Would I be with my partner, Paul? Most importantly, would I have my daughter, Clancy?

Here's the thing. I've learnt that you can't truly live when a regret is ruling your life. So while I am aware of these thoughts and the idea of what could have been, I've consciously embraced my life choices and owned the decision that was made for me back in 1971.

After my procedure, my parents and I spent a week in Queensland so I could rest and recover, which actually involved a whole lot of horrible cramping and contractions.

Looking back, I realise how smart Mum and Dad's moves were during this time. First, they didn't ban me from seeing John. What does an immature teen do if you tell them not to do something? They do it! I think my parents knew that if they made me break up with John, I would very much put my plan to run away to Perth back into action. Instead, they stepped back and let our relationship take its course.

The second thing they did was the perfect example of reverse psychology. As you'll recall, I had spectacularly failed my HSC. Feeling like I was capable of passing, I told my parents I wanted to repeat Year 12.

'Nah. You didn't care about it the first time, why would you care the second, Lynne?' Dad said. 'Just get a job and earn some money.'

Even though school hadn't been a burning passion of mine, I wanted my HSC and resorted to begging and cajoling Dad into letting me try again.

'It'll be different this time, I swear! I think I want to be a teacher. Let me move from Moorefield Girls' High to Blakehurst. Come on, it'll be a fresh start.'

As I say, Bruce McGranger was a clever man. I knew *he* wanted me to finish high school. I just didn't know that what he was doing was all to make *me* want to finish high school. After some more pleading, promise-making and orchestrating a very strong case, I was given his blessing and started Year 12 in February 1971 at Blakehurst High School.

For months afterwards, I'd wake up early to watch for John's flashing lights on the Princes Highway, but as I adjusted to my new life at Blakehurst, I couldn't help feeling like our paths were heading in different directions. My focus was on pleasing my parents and passing the HSC. I was also surprised by how seamlessly I slipped into the social scene at Blakehurst. Nobody knew anything about what had happened to me, which was how I liked it.

As far as high school experiences go, I lucked out by getting a year full of kind, accepting and bright kids and quickly hit it off with a group of guys with whom I'm still friends today. Everyone seemed to get along with everyone and even though we'd still use our free periods to go smoke cigarettes, drink Tab and play 500 or euchre at Derek's house, we somehow got some study done. While English was usually my strongest subject, suddenly I was reasonably good at maths too. Sadly not French ... which is weird because I felt like I had such an immersive experience moonlighting as Pascale. It could be that it was because we were all older, but I never felt like there were cliques at Blakehurst. Usually you have a big fish in a little pond or a little fish in a big pond, but at that school, everyone felt like equally sized fish.

Just like Year 5, Year 12 (well, the second time around) would prove to be memorable, largely thanks to a great teacher. Mr Spithonas had just come out of teachers' college, had long hippy hair and ran a folk music club. Needless to say, we all thought he was fabulous and desperately wanted to learn how to sing. I'd been hanging out with a girl named Debra and her sister Julia, both of whom came from the most bohemian family. This sounds pretty normal now, but at the time I was shocked that their parents would still be in bed while Debra and Julia made their own breakfast, packed their own bags and left for school. All on their own! I was even more dumbfounded when Julia would get out a box of Jatz and spread mashed avocado onto the crackers. I'd never eaten avocado in my life and couldn't help thinking, *Wow, this is so exotic!*

And Julia! This girl always seemed to be fostering cats and had no problem being alpha. I have a vivid memory of her biting a

47

feral cat on the paw after it got sassy with her. Oh and some guy once exposed himself to her on the train. In the first display of true girl power I'd ever seen, she just pointed and laughed. You know those WWJD bracelets everyone used to wear? I often think, *What Would Julia Do?*

But back to me wanting to sing. Debra could belt out a tune and could play guitar, so we'd spend many afternoons together practising songs like 'House of the Rising Sun' and 'If I Were a Carpenter'. We auditioned for Mr Spithonas and his folk music club and we both got in! As we sang our hearts out in the quad at school, I was keenly aware that after a long hard year, I had regained my mojo.

And yet in many ways, I was still incredibly naive.

Over the course of a few months, I noticed a girl putting on an awful lot of weight. She ended up leaving school for a while and when she came back, she was thin again. When discussing her magical weight-loss transformation (and hoping to discover her tips), a friend pointed out that she had clearly been pregnant and gone away to have a baby. How I missed this still baffles me to this day. I had just come out of a similar situation. If I'd known, I like to think I would have gone and talked to the girl about it.

As I continued to develop a sense of self and began thinking about what I was going to do after I left school, I realised there wasn't a tonne of room for John in my life anymore. While I still loved him, I'd stopped getting up to see those flashing lights and was aware that other men, friends and opportunities were becoming more important. I could also tell that John was distracted. We'd meet up at Sans Souci and sit in his car outside Lousy Les's, which was technically Mick Moylan's hotel, but the locals knew it as Lousy Les's. Anyway, we'd sit there crying and talking about our past and future. As much as we wanted to be together, we saw our lives heading in different directions. I didn't know it at the time, but John had found a girl – and God. Eventually I broke things off with him. Even though our love wasn't ever going to turn into a marriage with a house, kids and a dog, it was something that would stay with me forever.

My parents knew that going to Blakehurst and making new friends would spell the end of my relationship with John. I also feel like if I hadn't had that second chance to complete Year 12, I wouldn't have been able to cope with my accidental pregnancy and first heartbreak.

Every now and then I'd find sweet notes from John on my car's windscreen or in my mailbox. Nothing lovey-dovey, just simple words of encouragement, letting me know he was watching out for me and that he was proud of my choices. This went on for years. The last note I received was while I was doing an amateur performance of *How the Other Half Loves* at the Sutherland Civic Theatre. He'd stuck it under my windscreen wiper.

'Hope you're well. I always knew you were a great actress, Spud.'

To this day I wonder if John had seen me perform, or if he just knew I was appearing. Sadly, I can't ask him. In 1977, when I was twenty-four and he was just thirty, he was killed in a motorcycle accident. Mum broke the tragic news to me and asked if I wanted her to come to the funeral. The fact that she made it a point to find me quickly and tell me meant so much. But I ended up choosing to go alone. I sat quietly at the back of the chapel and watched his family, including his wife, mourn the man I had loved so much.

CHAPTER 5
Bye Bye Blakehurst, Hello Wagga

Aside from being banned from the school yearbook because I wore mascara on photo day, Blakehurst High was very good to me. It gave me the type of friendships you have for life, the confidence I needed to move on from John, and the motivation to continue my education.

After cleaning one too many fat vats while working at a Henny Penny chicken shop, I knew I needed a career away from the food industry (unless that career involved quality control in a Tim Tam factory). Actually, if I'd known being a food critic was a thing back then, I probably would have done that. I momentarily considered hairdressing, but couldn't stand the smell of the perming emulsion. Most girls I knew were doing nursing or a secretarial course, but the idea of changing someone's bedpan or being stuck in any sort of office setting for an extended period of time didn't do it for me.

I narrowed my options and settled on teachers' college. I know you're thinking, *This woman shouldn't be let anywhere near the youth of Australia. She'd probably eat all their lunches for starters* . . . It could have been Mr Sinclair or Miss Rapmund's influence, but funnily enough, standing in front of a captive audience for six or more hours a day appealed to the performer in me. Realistic about the fact that Sydney Uni wasn't an option with my marks, I ended up choosing to study in Wagga Wagga and moved down there in 1972.

One of the most exciting things about heading to Wagga Wagga Teachers' College, which had just changed to the Riverina College of Advanced Education (commonly known as Rivcol), was finding out which block of dormitories I would be living in. The whole month before the big move, countless questions went through my head. What would the common room set-up be? Would the bathrooms be gross? What type of snacks would be available on campus? But the question that lingered the most was: who would I be friends with? (Or as I would later teach my students, 'With whom would I be friends?')

At Blakehurst, my group had been a wonderfully decent and fun bunch of guys as well as Debra and a few other girls. I've always enjoyed male friendships so when I was told I'd be moving into X Block, I was hoping to create the same sort of mates and social life. As I scanned the fresh-faced students during Orientation Week, I noticed an abundance of men that I'll refer to here as the Hot Rugby Players. Smitten by their toned physiques, country boy charm, rough-around-the-edges humour and boundless confidence, I began imagining myself playing cards with them, laughing between classes, and maybe even making out.

As the unofficial poster-child for extroverts, I immediately inserted myself into every party, meet-up and communal kitchen chat I could find. Going streaking? Hold my top! Binge drinking behind the servo? I'm your girl! Smoking pot instead of studying? Sign me up!

But a few months went by and I started to experience feelings that can only be described as shame and loneliness. Instead of breaking into the cool clique and dazzling them with my wit and comedic timing, I came across as a try-hard and was left feeling like utter shit.

I didn't recognise this at the time, but it's clear now that the Hot Rugby Players simply didn't hold women in high esteem.

They were the type of men who let you get a little too drunk at a Bachelors and Spinsters Ball, if you know what I mean. While I never found myself doing the walk of shame covered in mud from a paddock party, I did wind up in the shower trying to get the horrific stench of tomato sauce, liniment, and God knows what else out of my hair.

The details of how I came to be in the following situation are blurry, but I'm pretty sure I was dared to let the Hot Rugby Players throw me fully clothed into a bath of sludge. We'd been in the common room drinking and I remember feeling intimidated by a stunning Swedish girl named Helene. With legs for days and the type of crystalline blue eyes you want to snorkel in, I knew that I would have to rely on my personality if I was going to outshine this Nordic beauty. *She might be beautiful, but is she fun?* I thought as four manly men hoisted my body into a bath filled with a mixture of liquids no living thing should ever be submerged in.

At the time, I thought I was being wild, carefree and a good sport. But with the benefit of hindsight, I know that there was a degree of malice attached to the Hot Rugby Players' actions that makes my heart break for College Lynne. I was naive and easy prey. Sadly, it took a few more months of me drinking myself into oblivion and sleeping with guys who didn't like me back before I requested to be moved to a new dorm in W Block. Sometimes, you need a geographical cure.

Even though I've always been a bit of a pack animal, I decided to switch up my 'quest for acceptance' strategy when I changed dorms. First things first: I needed to get my weight under control because my excessive drinking and late night eating hadn't been kind to my waistline. Nearly every weekend, half a dozen of the Hot Rugby Players' groupies, myself included, would pile into my Fiat 650 rice bubble of a car in the wee hours and drive to Daisy's, the local greasy spoon truck stop, and feast on toasted cheese sangas. Equal parts illegal and impressive, we must have looked like we were trying to win an act in the Great Moscow Circus.

Anyway, this behaviour was one of the many reasons I started upping my daily dose of Ford Pills to around sixteen tablets. Don't worry – I had switched from the standard Ford Pills to their natural senna version, which was healthier ... right? Next, I focused on making friends with people one at a time. Early on, I met Jenny, who was a bit of a leveller for me. When I would be tempted to jump on a literal bandwagon and do something questionable, she'd politely point out why parading through campus in a flimsy nightie at 2 a.m. on a balmy three-degree Tuesday wasn't a great idea. She also told me about the Rivcol Drama Club. Up until that point, I hadn't really done much performing, other than singing in Mr Spithonas' folk music club, a school play here and there and of course my dazzling backyard

My Fair Lady performances as a seven-year-old … but the drama club sounded like it had my name written all over it.

During the club's first meeting of the year, I met Colin R. Anderson, the head of the college drama department. Roughly fifteen years older than me, Colin had moved down from Newcastle as part of a decentralising initiative the state was running to get more people to live and work regionally. Standing five foot two inches high, I don't think Colin could have weighed more than fifty kilograms soaking wet. But while he may have been physically small, his personality and talents were larger than life. Today you might describe him as 'camp' or 'flamboyant', but back then you'd simply say he was gayer than your pet unicorn.

Colin was the first openly gay man I had ever met, which wasn't surprising for the early 1970s. I loved how comfortable he was about his sexuality and watched him help other men, like Bobby Fields, come out over the years. On my first day in the drama club, I also met Lynne Cooper, who would quickly become my non-sexual soulmate. Lynne had an in with what seemed like every group. She was a little bit theatre, a little bit music and a whole lot of fun. Like Jenny, Lynne made me feel confident and comfortable.

The first performance the drama club did was a revue called *The Biodegradable, Strictly Non-Fadable, Nothing Synthetic, Nothing*

Magnetic, Nothing Inflated, Poly-Unsaturated, Unpolluted REVUE ... It's Organically Grown. Lynne and I created a sketch called *The Bitches.* Loosely scripted, we'd wander through the audience portraying a couple of older bitchy gasbags named Blanche and Ruby and basically pick on the audience. I modelled my character, Blanche, after a suburban housewife-cum-gossip who loved nothing more than sitting on people's laps while delivering mild insults and come-ons.

At this point in time, all of Wagga seemed to come to our shows so we had doctors, lawyers and even the mayor, Richard Gorman, to rouse on. I don't know if we were particularly funny or not, but we did become a bit famous. On opening night, we had around 350 people in the audience. Mayor Gorman even told the local paper, 'It's the best thing I've seen for years.' (Obviously, he needed to get out more.) While that review filled me with pride, what mattered most was that I finally felt like I belonged.

When it came time to audition for the club's major performance of the year, *Bye Bye Birdie,* I proudly took the stage, sang and acted my heart out and was awarded the role of Rosie DeLeon, the very part Janet Leigh had played in the film. Getting to spend my time rehearsing with the drama club resulted in so many positive things. For starters, I lost weight and I swear it wasn't from abusing laxatives. I think it was a combination of dance rehearsals and having less downtime to snack. Whatever it was, I was grateful that I was still able to indulge in my morning tea ritual, which involved chocolate milk and a cinnamon roll.

I also met Darryl, who was and is as mad as a cut snake. He was in loads of performances with me and eventually became my boyfriend. (More on Darryl later.) When my parents heard I was going to be in *Bye Bye Birdie*, they took the train down to see my performance. My mum got such a kick out of watching me onstage after all those years of me reciting *My Fair Lady* in our lounge room. While acting was just something they thought I was doing for fun while in college, I could sense their pride and approval.

I also received praise from Colin R. Anderson, arguably the most talented parody writer in the world, which put a spring in my step that carried me through production after production.

Next, I auditioned for *Orpheus in the Underworld*. The lead roles in this play required proper voices aka voices that don't sound like they've chain-smoked a pack of Winnie Blues a day for twenty years, so I was cast in the chorus and loved every minute of it. Over the next couple of years, I couldn't get enough of the drama scene.

On top of participating in the Rivcol Drama Club, I branched out into the Wagga Wagga School of the Arts and performed in a few productions there. Although my marks weren't great, I was enjoying my classes and most importantly – passing. Except for art. (I'd failed colouring-in in kindergarten, so this didn't come as a shock.)

On top of those wonderful things, my relationship with my family had never been stronger. One holidays while back home, my seventeen-year-old sister Paula announced she'd fallen in love with Peter … who was ready to get married. Peter didn't want Paula to work and to be honest, Paula didn't want Paula to work, so she was thinking of giving up studying. She'd planned to become a nurse. Needless to say, Dad was beside himself. Feeling sad for her, I went and explained that Peter loved Paula so much and would move heaven and earth for her. I then firmly suggested that Dad not get in her way. I'm glad I interjected because Peter and Paula are still together. (And yes, she'll proudly tell you she's never worked a day in her life.)

My sister's love life might have been blossoming, but mine, on the other hand, was a little bit rockier. I'd met a new guy, James, when I moved to yet another dorm, this time in A Block. Even though the two most accurate words to describe James may have been 'portly' and 'hairy', I was infatuated. It was most likely because he showed no interest in me whatsoever, except for the time he decided to bring to my attention the fact that I had 'a really odd body'. (Um, hello pot kettle black.)

My obsession with James, his insults and his nightly routine of listening to the cricket for hours on end even led me to turn down Michael Holmes, who was working backstage on the production of *West Side Story* I was in. Thrilled to be playing the part of Anita and getting to pick the brains of Colin yet again, it took me longer than usual to notice that Michael, who had long hair and was musically gifted, was a total catch. I mean, who wants to date the wildly talented musician who actually likes you when you could have a real life Hairy Maclary posing as a brutally honest Magic Mirror? Thankfully, my other A Block friends, Gay and Beth, helped me come to my senses. After Pep Talk number 297, I decided to leave James and his cricket-listening, knocked on Michael's door and said, 'Let's do this.'

Over the next year I fell in love. It was similar to the love I had felt for John Gilmour, but it went even deeper. I think because I was older, Michael and I connected on a higher emotional level. I simply couldn't get enough of him. He came home with me to Sydney for my twenty-first birthday, where my Uncle Bill proceeded to get so drunk, he forgot to put film in the camera. The only picture I have from the night is one of Michael and me cutting the cake.

I'm not saying that I was envisioning a wedding dress, tuxedo and church bells every time I was with Michael, but I definitely thought we were a forever type deal. That's why when I sensed that he was pulling back, I spiralled into complete panic mode.

Suddenly I didn't trust him, I didn't trust other women and I could barely focus on anything but Michael and our relationship.

I'm not proud of what I'm about to tell you next, but there's no other way to say it. While stalking him one evening, I followed him to a flat. I watched him get off his bike, walk up some stairs and then *kiss* Elizabeth Star on the mouth before pulling her inside. Confident this wasn't an impromptu tutorial in mouth-to-mouth resuscitation, I prepared myself for quite the confrontation when he was done doing whatever he was doing. Unfortunately, night fell and I needed to go home and sleep, which was obviously going to be impossible knowing that Michael and Elizabeth were together.

Somehow, I managed to make it through the night and only develop a slight eye twitch due to exhaustion. When I tracked down Michael the next day, he was so matter of fact about his lack of love for me that it left me broken. Unlike the way my relationship with John Gilmour ended, which had been gradual, beautiful and essentially a story of star-crossed lovers, Michael ripped me from his life like a kid discards Christmas wrapping paper.

As I was left lying in a puddle of my own tears, he rode off into the sunset with mother-effing Elizabeth Star. Did I perpetuate every stereotype about a woman scorned? Yes, I did. Did I hit a new record for kilojoules consumed post-heartbreak? You bet.

Did I sink into so deep a depression that my friends considered hiring a crane to get me out? Yep. Luckily, they didn't need a crane. My A Block saviours, Gay and Beth, along with my drama club mates, Lynne, Jenny, Darryl and even Colin, were able to help me find my feet and get back in the game.

I eventually got over Michael, but still to this day, I can't listen to a Moody Blues album without thinking of him.

But don't worry – there was redemption.

Years down the track, I ran into Elizabeth Star at a party. We talked about what had happened. She'd long since moved on and was highly apologetic for unintentionally being the other woman. But she had some good news for me. These days, Michael has no teeth. We both dodged a bullet.

After leaving my mark on X Block, W Block and A Block, I made the decision to move off campus with Darryl and a guy named Brownie. I'm grateful to be here writing this today because living with Brownie was like living with Mr Bean. While he was a dyed-in-the-wool hippy who radiated peace, love and patchouli-scented farts, the man made my entire family look like Michelin starred chefs.

On more than one occasion I found him trying to deep-fry

peas and boil an egg – without water. While his approach to cooking was like watching a toddler try to drink from an overly full glass, the worst thing he did was put water in Darryl's Birko Jug food warmer and then forget about it. Within hours it had melted through the laminex in the kitchen and was wafting waves of toxic VOC-filled smoke through all two storeys of our flat. Every single item in our home – clothing, cushions, even cutlery – reeked of smoke and plastic. How it didn't burst into flames, I'll never know.

Luckily, our landlord was insured and Brownie didn't manage to nearly burn the place down ever again. Well, if he did, I was too busy to notice because when I wasn't studying, I was rehearsing for my latest role in Brian Friel's *Lovers: Winners and Losers* or hanging out with Lynne and the bikies of Wagga Wagga.

As someone who has always adopted the 'when in Rome' approach to life experiences, of course I started dating one of the bikies, Jinx. Jinx earnt himself this cute nickname because watching him go through life was like watching someone set off all the booby traps in an Indiana Jones movie – at once. Jinx was fun, but I was mostly there to hang with Lynne and her bikie boyfriend as well as smoke as much dope as I could get my hands on.

While I definitely think there was an opportunity here for me to dive deep into the Wagga Wagga bikie scene and adopt some major Gemma Teller from *Sons of Anarchy* vibes, my love and commitment to the drama club kept a hold on me. Sort of. I do recall sitting in a bikie bar one afternoon and watching a gang of burly wind-blown men saunter through the door with a paper-wrapped package that resembled what you get when you order takeaway fish and chips. As I watched Lynne's boyfriend unwrap it, I was shocked to see a huge block of weed instead of twenty fish cocktails and chicken-salt-covered chips.

By this point, I felt like I could really handle smoking dope, but I don't know what strain this was because after a few tokes, Lynne and I started laughing and did not stop for twelve hours. My abs were on fire. My jaw was aching. Tears streaked my cheeks. As we walked arm in arm home that night, it must have been around 1 or 2 a.m., we accidentally fell into somebody's hedge. After vacillating between snort-laughter and maniacal cackles, we finally caught our breath and had a moment of silence, which was quickly broken by Lynne's obscenely loud declaration ... 'It smells like sperm!'

And just like that we were back laughing.

To this day I can't look at a neatly trimmed hedge without thinking of the scent of sperm.

I also know I've never done a better abdominal workout in my life.

Bikie shenanigans aside, once I got cast as Margaret Mary

Enright aka Mag in the *Winners* part of *Lovers*, I knew I would need to work extra hard to capture the Irish accent and ultimately do the character justice, which meant less dope smoking with the bikies. Thankfully, our wonderful director, Betty Herr, was a mistress of accents and coached us brilliantly. I don't know if you've ever watched or read *Lovers: Winners and Losers*, but the *Winners* part of the play is actually quite poignant and has a storyline that was not too dissimilar to my own: an unexpected teen pregnancy and difficult life choices.

Because the show was part of the Wagga Wagga School of Arts Players 1974 Drama Festival (a big deal in the amateur theatre world), on the morning before the performance, I received a telegram from Colin which read, 'May winners be just that.' His support, encouragement, enthusiasm, friendship and talent has never stopped influencing me. I just wish he was still here so he could read this.

If there's one thing that I've learnt about acting, it's draw from past experience when you can. You're the only tool you've got. The other important thing is never to place too much importance on reviews: there will always be people who love what you do and others who'd rather drink a cup of cold sick than watch you perform.

The *Winners* review in the *Wagga Wagga Advertiser* was kind of kind, very brief and certainly accurate.

'Lynne McGranger depicted a teenage girl's love and fear of the future.'

Before I knew it, the festival had nominated me for Best Individual Performance (Actress) for my portrayal of Mag. In an article in the college paper, dear Colin had pegged me or an older actress from the Canberra Repertory Workshop for the gong. Of course I wanted to win, but I was just so damned chuffed to be in the same category as Margaret de Mestre, who had blown me away with her performance in *One Season's King*.

On the day of the awards, my friend and co-star, Mark Ellerman, was awarded Most Promising Actor. Colin had picked this too. Next came the Best Actress Award. It's all a bit of a blur now, but they called out my name. I'd won. Convinced it was a mistake, it took me a full fifteen seconds to will myself to walk to the stage to accept the perpetual trophy, which had my name engraved on it. Spelt correctly! Plus a little personal trophy, which I still have.

As I managed to make noises that resembled talking, I thanked my peers for such a validating award. I then raced around to Lynne Cooper's place and we celebrated. For the first time in my life I thought that maybe I was okay at this acting thing. My parents, who had come down to watch the show on opening night, were also thinking the same thing. Shortly after winning the award, I received a sweet card from my mum.

> *To Dear Lynne,*
> *Who knows! We may have a Bette Davis in the family yet! Just thought we'd congratulate you once more on your success.*
> *Love,*
> *Mum, Dad and Paula*

After the festival ended, it was time to focus on finishing my last semester of teachers' college. This was proving quite difficult because I had just moved into a new share house with two girls, Wendy and Kim, and a chef named Carl. We hit it off with a couple, Simon and Cynthia, and their two teenage kids who lived across the street. Together, we'd play cards literally all night. I'm not exaggerating. I didn't learn a lot at college, but boy could I play canasta. I'd leave there at 8.45 a.m., have a quick shower and then barely make it to my first lecture. This probably explains why once again my marks weren't great.

Simon and Cynthia's relationship seemed so exotic because they were in an open marriage. Being brutally honest, I had a fling with Simon. He told me Cynthia knew. I'm not so sure. Sadly, their marriage didn't survive its openness, but my friendship with Cynthia did.

There was something else that happened at this time that explains why I couldn't focus. Remember Bobby Fields? The guy Colin helped come out? During the Winter Frolic Ball, he went into his garage and sat in his running car, along with his dog. Friends got wind of his plans and came round to check on him. They sat him down, talked it out, took his keys and were convinced he was fine.

Turns out he had another set of keys.

His death was an utter tragedy. It made me start thinking about the importance of mental health. He was just twenty-one.

☆ ☆ ☆

At last, I graduated from Rivcol and was on my way back home to be a teacher at Lugarno Public School in Sydney's south. Even though my friend Lynne had graduated the year before, farewelling my other mates and drama club life was hard. These years were hands down some of the most fun and rewarding of my life and having to leave without knowing if my next chapter would involve performing sucked. But like always, Colin knew exactly what to say. Packaged with a beautiful copper chalice, he sent me the following note:

For the Magnificent, Marvellous McGranger . . .
May you drink deep from this cup in memory of what was and in
anticipation of all that is to come. My admiration of your talent,
my appreciation of your friendship, my joy of having you around
– there are no bounds to any of them.
With love and gratitude,
Colin

Rest in peace, my friend.

CHAPTER 6
Adulting Away and at Home

Have you ever spent nearly four years of your life studying something only to discover you have absolutely no interest in the profession? When I graduated and moved back home with my parents, at last ready to take my new career seriously, I was surprised by how much I was dreading the first day as a Year 4 teacher. Wearing my favourite I'd-like-to-command-your-attention outfit (red miniskirt, black tights and a black sweater), I entered the school grounds feeling like I really looked the part of a teacher. (If said teacher were equal parts eccentric and out-there.) Now the question was – could I play it?

Since old habits die hard, I concentrated on making teacher friends before figuring out how to connect with the curious little faces in my class. This is when I met Lynette Matthews, who informed me that she would 'rip my effing tits off' if I ever called her by her full name. So I will refer to her as 'Lyn with one n' as I'm rather attached to my mammaries. Lyn and I miraculously made it through the first school year thanks in part to our mutual love of witty banter, toasted muffins with Peck's Paste and poached eggs, travel and taking full advantage of our sick leave.

Most of all, we loved taking the piss out of each other when on playground duty. Since this was the 1970s, we'd take drags of our cigarettes while telling kids to 'Go ask Mrs Matthews to show you her AC/DC tattoo.' Awestruck at the thought of a tattooed teacher, they'd excitedly run off to ask to see it. Of course they'd always come back asking to see my ABBA underwear.

One of the biggest mistakes I made before choosing teachers' college was not spending time with any kids to make sure I actually enjoyed their company. Turns out that when children are in groups of more than one, they make me nervous. While the kindies are cute, trying to teach them to read is about as thrilling as ... well, trying to teach them to read. The older ones were okay, I suppose, as long as they weren't smuggling in alcohol or dealing dope. Eleven-year-olds can be very resourceful.

When I wasn't confiscating bottles of whiskey and foils of weed, I enjoyed chatting with Wayne Chin. He was a Year 5 teacher and made me laugh. This was one of those rare situations when I knew a guy liked me more than I liked him. The evidence: he proposed after six weeks of dating when I was still perfectly fine chatting up other men. I considered his proposal because he was kind and we got on, but we were lacking the passion couples should have for at least – I don't know, the first week. Also, since it didn't occur to me at the time that I could keep my own surname, the idea of going through life as 'Lynne Chin' made my decision even easier. No offence, Wayne.

You can see why after breaking a co-worker's heart and having a plethora of parents wanting me to tell them how special their children were, I was desperate to get away for the summer holidays. 'Lyn with one n' suggested we book a Russian cruise ship to New Zealand via Fiji, New Caledonia and Vanuatu. Great idea! Before you could say *budem zdorovi*, we were all aboard the *Fyodor Shalyapin*. In my head, we were setting sail on a grand ship to spend fourteen days drenched in sun, cocktails and male attention. I'd come back to school feeling reinvigorated and fresh for the next year.

Turns out Cyclone Elsa had other plans.

Shortly after leaving Sydney Harbour, the *Fyodor Shalyapin*, complete with absolutely *no* stabilisers, encountered the type of weather that makes you really take note of where the life jackets and lifeboats are. I felt less like a cruise ship passenger and more like a cork in Bass Strait. The one positive thing about the gale force winds was that they were the most effective way of losing weight I've ever found! I shed six kilograms in twelve days without using laxatives because I could not stop vomiting. The only thing I could keep down was the truly tasteless cheese and tomato sandwiches (don't Russians have salt mines?), which I'd nibble during the late dining seating. As soon as I finished, I ran in a manner similar to an ostrich (fast, low and with a little junk in the trunk) to my room, which was one of those cheap, windowless, middle-of-the-ship cabins you have to share with strangers.

Once inside, everything I did needed to be in a horizontal position to ensure I didn't spew yet another bland excuse for a Russian delicacy. This was slightly difficult when it came to showering because the shower was less than a metre around. Essentially in the foetal position, I'd have to rotate my body like human clock hands to fully suds and rinse my surface area. Once clean, I would crawl into bed and lie on a towel as I air-dried. Once suitable for clothing, I'd summon the magical powers Mum had bestowed upon me and dress myself while lying down.

This whole routine was made all the more awkward because I'd have to ask my stranger cabin mates to leave the room until I was done. Yet another confession: I don't think the cyclone was the only reason for my intense nausea. One of the drawcards of the discount Russian cruise was that being in international waters meant access to cheap cigarettes, vodka and Bacardi rum.

After about my eighth night of observing just how fast my body could regurgitate food and alcohol, I recall lying on a bench on the top deck desperate for the sea air to soothe me. Bracing myself as the waves broke over the bridge, I looked up to the sky and said out loud, 'God, take me now. I can't do this anymore.' While He didn't end my misery right there and then, the Sky Boss did help us reach New Zealand. To this day, I'm not sure if we docked or washed ashore. Needless to say, this was the first and last cruise I ever went on.

Suddenly Lugarno Public wasn't looking so bad.

☆ ☆ ☆

Safely back on dry land, I spent a bit of time with my family before gearing up for the second year of school. Since it was clear teaching was never going to feed my creative side, I started taking some drama classes and participating in amateur theatre. My first show was *How the Other Half Loves* by British playwright Alan Ayckbourn, at the Cronulla School of Arts, where one night an electrical blackout meant we performed the entire second act in the dark. Oh the joys of community theatre! I was cast as Teresa Phillips and had a ball.

After Cronulla, we took the play to the Sutherland Civic Theatre – the very one where John Gilmour left that note on my car. Even though it was an amateur production, we received some good press and reviews. My personal favourite was titled 'Husky' and began, 'Lynne McGranger has some gorgeous husky qualities in her voice …' Flying high from all the praise in the *Cronulla Gazette*, I immediately bought a pack of cigarettes and started looking for the next gig.

Since there weren't a tonne of shows for me to audition for, I enrolled in as many workshops as possible, which led me to reconnect with mad-as-a-cut-snake Darryl, who had moved back to Sydney from Wagga Wagga. For some reason, 1976 made Darryl look pretty good and we started dating. By dating I mean we were friends with benefits, which is why it was okay when my eyes wandered a bit when I was in Armidale for a drama workshop in January 1977. And wander they did to a ridiculously handsome art teacher by the name of Peter. Originally from Tamworth, I learnt that Peter was living and teaching in Sydney (only minutes away!) and, best of all, he was single. Since he showed no interest in me, I proceeded to make it my mission to gain his attention and affection. It took a few weeks of constant badgering and luring him into my room with my undeniable sex appeal, but eventually Peter seemed to be on the same page as me and we were officially official.

For a good few months, I felt like a bona fide adult. I had a cute boyfriend, a good job, and I paid my bills ... sometimes. But there was something missing ... theatre. While I had always thought of performing as more of a hobby, I began to notice that my days and weekends felt dull if I wasn't either rehearsing or performing. Nothing made me feel more alive than curtains opening, stage lights warming my skin and the sound of an audience laughing, gasping or offering an empathetic sigh right on cue.

While on the hunt for another show to audition for, I stumbled upon an advertisement for a workshop in Hurstville. Thrilled to be back in my element, this experience led to an invitation to join the Q Theatre, originally a lunchtime theatre group that met in the old AMP building in the city. Under the guidance of Doreen Warburton, it moved to Penrith, otherwise known as Sydney's 'cultural wasteland' at the time. The plan was to increase the number of productions and add evening shows.

After being given the old Railway Institute Building, Doreen and the genius minds of Kevin Jackson, Arthur Dicks and Richard Brooks, along with all of us workshop participants, built and upholstered the audience seating, painted acres of walls, sewed stage curtains and basically put our blood, sweat and tears into what became the rather famous Q Theatre we know today. Well, it's actually been knocked down and since rebuilt as the Joan Sutherland Performing Arts Centre, but for decades it was called the Q and was a beacon for up-and-coming actors like Toni Collette, Judy Davis (and Lynne McGranger).

Once the renovation was complete, our first production was *Lock Up Your Daughters*, a musical adaptation of Henry Fielding's 1730 play, *Rape upon Rape*. (I wonder why they changed the name …) I played a whalebone-corset-wearing maid and here's the best part: I got paid. I also got to join Actors Equity, which – kind of, sort of – felt like I had made it in life. While it was surreal to be part of Actors Equity, I mostly just couldn't believe I was getting money for doing something I loved. Even Peter was impressed that I was earning upwards $100 a week from a side hustle!

Over the next few months, I played Minnie Symperson in W.S. Gilbert's *Engaged* and Anne Marten in *The Murder of Maria Marten*. (Ka-ching, ka-ching.) The extra money was really helpful because my friend, Linda, whom I'd met at teachers' college in Wagga Wagga, and I had been saving to go to the UK for a bit of a gap year. Like most of the plans I make in life, our overseas adventure itinerary was loose, but as 1978 approached and our bank accounts steadily grew bigger, we realised it was the right time to book our flights. Would I say the timing was perfect in terms of how things were going with my boyfriend Peter and the Q? No. But I knew travelling wasn't something I wanted to miss out on and I believed both Peter and the Q would be there when I got back. With that mindset and a jam-packed suitcase, Linda June and I set off for London on New Year's Day 1978.

I suspect a lot of girls embark on a backpacking trip hoping to get cinnamon-coloured skin, natural highlights and the faint outline of a six-pack from carrying their belongings around. Even though I knew I was headed to London in January – in the middle of winter – for some reason, I still kept imagining myself lounging on a boat off the Italian riviera or wandering through grape vines in Bordeaux ...

It was not to be. We navigated the tube into the city from Heathrow and found our pre-arranged bed and breakfast in Paddington. When an army of cockroaches opened the door for us, took our bags and even performed turndown service, it's safe to say my Mediterranean idyll was well and truly crushed. But as a backpacker on a budget, you take what you can get ... even if it means a filthy bed and breakfast run by a portly man named Lindsay with a very impressive mullet.

Dear Peter,   *8 January 1978*

We've made it! I'm in London. No, the bed and breakfast looks nothing like the pictures, but we've met two lovely Australian girls who've been here for three months and lived to tell about it. One of the girls is named Jill and she's from Tassie. You wouldn't believe it – her parents were in a car during the Tasman Bridge collapse that just happened a few days ago! They were teetering on the edge about to plunge to their deaths when a rescue team winched them to safety. WILD. Jill is really shook up, but not going to cut her trip short. The other girl is Annie and she's from Melbourne. Annie's been in the UK for nearly a year and has given Linda and me so much advice. Our first trip is going to be skiing in Austria. I know, I know ... I've never even seen snow, but there's got to be a first time for everything, right? I also heard about jobs going at the Queen Elizabeth Hotel. Heading there tomorrow. How are you? I miss you madly. We need to come here together someday. Please write soon.

Love,

Lynne

As I awaited Peter's reply, I started work as a waitress at the aforementioned Queen Elizabeth Hotel. While no, I didn't have much experience either serving people or pouring people drinks,

I was *very* familiar with fermented beverages and banter so I fitted right in.

Even though Australia is part of the Commonwealth, I couldn't believe how different London felt. Its age, its history and of course the continual shenanigans of the Royal Family were astonishing. Every day I devoured stories from old buildings, the exhaust from double-decker buses and of course that famous English breakfast – Vegemite on toast. While I would have loved to have swan dived into a plate of eggs, bacon, sausage, black pudding, baked beans and fried toast, I was on a very strict budget.

One morning while walking to my shift, I was nearly taken down and dragged through the cobblestone streets by a man on horseback. *What on earth was that?* I slowly peeled my body off the sandstone wall I had tried to become one with in an effort to save my life. Turns out, Prince Edward had just galloped by! Suddenly my near death didn't seem so bad.

At work, I told everyone who would listen about how Prince Edward and his fine steed had nearly taken me out. Overnight my tale evolved to include him bandaging me up and us riding off into the sunset together. As they say – never let the truth get in the way of a good story.

The maître d' at the hotel, Klaus, seemed to find me and my antics amusing. No matter how many times I tried to look busy and hint that I was very much in love with my boyfriend

Peter back in Australia, he found a reason to pull me aside and cajole me in his thick German accent. After weeks of asking me to accompany him to dinner, I finally gave in and agreed to go to a French restaurant. As you'll recall, I failed French miserably in high school, which was not ideal because this was the type of French restaurant where they only spoke French.

As Klaus and the waiter chatted away, I plastered one of those smiles on my face that says, 'I have no idea what you're saying, but I'm trying not to look bored and annoyed.' I also silently recoiled every time Klaus tried to rub his foot against my leg. On the walk home, he continued to stand a little too close, crowding my personal space, and seemed adamant about coming up to my room. I was in love with Peter and even if I wasn't, Klaus was not someone I wanted to explore feelings or bodies with. As we stood on the bed and breakfast doorstep, I did my best to bid him goodnight, but his inward lean was telling me that he had no intentions of going home. How on earth were the following social cues not resonating?

'I'm really tired. Thanks for dinner.'

'I can't wait to sleep alone tonight.'

'I better get inside and go to bed. *Alone.*'

By the grace of God, the portly bed and breakfast proprietor Lindsay opened the front door ... in his underwear. Never in my life have I been so grateful to see a pantless man with a prize-winning belly and a mullet blowing in a gust of wind. Klaus was seemingly put off and finally left after Lindsay gave him the stink eye.

Clearly, I had to quit my job at the hotel to avoid further awkward encounters, which was fine because Linda and I had worked out an arrangement with Lindsay similar to Jill and Anne's where we could clean the bathrooms and make breakfast in exchange for room and board.

I also tried my hand at collating a mail out, but the machine that spun the folder paper around gave me such extreme motion sickness that it made my little jaunt on the *Fyodor Shalyapin* feel like a day at the spa. I only lasted one hour.

While saving for my next trip, Linda, Jill, Anne and two new friends, Keith and Des, developed a morning cycle of breakfast, bath and a bowl (of dope). Any hopes of me getting that six-pack were quickly fading because let's be honest – a bowl of porridge looks like chocolate cake when you're stoned.

One day I received a letter from Colin Schumacher, who was helping produce a performance of *The Rocky Horror Picture Show* in Wagga Wagga for the Riverina Trucking Company. Apparently the casting team wanted me to play Magenta. Of all the roles I would have given my right arm to play, Magenta was definitely one of them!

But as much as I wanted to don fishnet stockings and a maid's

uniform, I didn't want to sacrifice the rest of my trip. On top of
exploring the UK, I had booked a ten-week European bus tour
with Keith as well as a week-long cruise of the Greek Islands. So
I politely declined. (That said, I'm still very keen to play Magenta
and if anyone wants to help me produce a geriatric version with
the cast in their sixties and seventies, I'm your girl!) Sad that the
show was literally going on without me, I wrote to Peter.

Dear Peter,   *7 June 1978*
*Hello from rainy London! Even though the weather is dreary,
it's still so exciting to be in such a bustling city with fun friends. I
got offered the part of Magenta in Rocky Horror in Wagga that's
opening in August. Sadly, I turned it down and they ended up
giving the part to Janette Crowe. I'm bummed to miss out, but
looking forward to heading to Paris with Keith. How are things
with you? How's school? I know you must be busy, but please try
to write a bit more!*
Lots of love,
Lynne

As the weather warmed up and my savings were looking good,
Keith and I headed to the continent. Kind, loyal and ex-military,
this guy was like a nuggety blond version of Liam Neeson. He
was from Newcastle, Australia, and had lied about his age to

Mum and Dad on their honeymoon at Kiama beach NSW, December 1948.

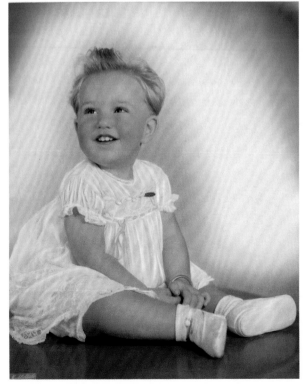

Me, rocking the hair at about nine months.

Dad, Paula and me in
Melbourne, circa 1958.

Even at age five, my fashion
sense was there for all to see
(please note the socks and
sandals and the buttoned-up
cardy under my cowgirl vest).

Paula (on right) and me at about three and seven years old, proudly wearing the matching merry-go-round dresses that Mum slaved over.

Graduation from the Riverina College of Advanced Education (aka Rivcol), Wagga 1975. I don't know what's going on with my face here, but I was always proud of my skinny pins (thanks, Mum!).

Paula, her then fiancé (now husband) Peter, an old school chum John Watson and me, circa 1976. Not sure where we were going or why Paula didn't get the memo about it being formal.

School days. Apparently I trained these girls to a netball premiership – who knew? Pictured here with the Principal, Mr O'Brien (we're both probably holding sneaky ciggies behind our backs).

Birthday with the then BF, circa 1977. Good grief, so much crimped hair and those Farrah Fawcett wings!

College review days/leader of the pack promo/scaring the locals in Wagga Wagga.
Left to right: me, Nancy Adams, Lynne Cooper and Janette Crowe.

Q Theatre days. *The Murder of Maria Marten*, November 1977. The fabulous Linden Wilkinson despairs at my overacting.

Q Theatre again. Eilis O'Beirne, yours truly and David Wheeler in *Paradise Regained*, November 1979.

That hair and make-up course I took certainly paid off! Miss Damina in the 'Pinteresque' *Don't Just Lie There, Say Something!* at the Bankstown Civic Centre, June 1980.

The *Natural Normans* minus the spectacular Denise Scott, so I'm guessing this was at the Edinburgh Festival 1989 (with Lynda Gibson and Sally-Anne Upton).

get into the army so he could fight in the Vietnam War ... at sixteen! Almost twenty-two by the time of our trip, I felt extra safe bouncing from city to city with him as my ally. Over ten weeks we explored Austria, Switzerland, Bulgaria, Yugoslavia and Croatia.

This was during the time of the Iron Curtain and when we went to Bulgaria, our guide had to bribe the border patrol guard with ABBA cassette tapes. Who knew the iconic Swedish pop group would be such great currency? Once safely behind the curtain, our first stop was St Sophia Church in the eponymous capital city. While I wasn't great about going to church on a regular basis back home, I did feel a connection to my faith and God and was looking forward to seeing such a historic and holy site.

Grateful for the opportunity, I was quickly distracted by two older women with squinty eyes, scrunched up noses and saliva flying from their pursed lips. Dear God – they were spitting on me. Appalled and confused, I turned to our tour guide, who explained the women were upset that my top didn't have sleeves. Unaware that there was a dress code, a kind priest offered me his jacket so that I could enter the church. Inside, the intricate brick archways kept my chin to the sky the entire time. I was in complete awe of the structure and wandered around for over an hour before taking a seat on a pew. I sat in silence thinking about how lucky I was to be in Bulgaria, and how blessed I was to have Peter and my family at home waiting for me. I made a prayer request to have a chance to keep acting when the trip ended.

Sometimes Keith and I slummed it in tents, other times we stayed in posh ski lodges. It didn't matter what the accommodation was, I didn't want to be anywhere else in the world. Except for the one time I took one too many laxatives (turns out my max for a day is twenty) and had to stray from the group and shit in a cornfield. I let out a battle cry of gratitude for making it to a somewhat private row of corn stalks. I considered that maybe laxatives weren't a good idea anymore.

On the other hand, I'd put on nearly twenty kilograms since arriving in the UK ... imagine how heavy I would be if I hadn't taken them at all. Since misery loves company, it made me feel better that all of the other girls had put on weight too. It got to the point where every time we wanted to wear our jeans, we'd have to lie on a bed and use a wire coat hanger to try to pull the zipper up. How we didn't render ourselves infertile, I'll never know.

Public defecation and muffin tops aside, one of my favourite parts of the trip was visiting the coastline along the Adriatic Sea. I don't know what the blokes are eating over there, but they are next level gorgeous! Even though I was tempted by toned men offering me carafes of wine and bowls of marinated olives, I stayed true to Peter and went back to London committed and in love.

But something odd happened when I got back to the bed and breakfast … suddenly Des was very flirty. His dirty-blond hair was very Robert Redford while his clothes screamed prep school. Within a few days he'd swept me off my feet and whisked me away to York where he gave me a White Rose of York. I was honest with him that I had Peter waiting for me at home, but he just held my gaze so intently, I couldn't help but feel what he was feeling too. In my head, I wondered if it was just that intense love you only feel on holiday or if there was something more to our connection. I decided I wouldn't make a choice until I had gone home and seen Peter.

When Linda and I planned our UK adventure, we figured we'd stay for about a year. But as autumn approached, I knew I was ready to get back to earning decent money, participating in the theatre and feeling Peter's warm embrace. I wrote to him one last time telling him about my plans to come home early. He agreed to pick me up at the airport. When I exited the international terminal, I expected to see him clutching flowers, an ecstatic smile on his face. Instead, I saw a look that clearly said, 'Who is this *enormous* woman who apparently ate Lynne?' I get it – I was fat. (Which is a word I really don't like.) But his demeanour had changed so drastically, I started to think maybe it was more than my weight that he didn't like.

We drove to my mum and dad's house to surprise them. Unlike my superficial boyfriend, my parents looked at me with the kind of love and acceptance that instantly makes you feel safe. Oh how I had missed them.

As I nursed what I thought was jetlag over the next few weeks, I found it surprisingly difficult to get in touch with Peter. He seemed to be busy with 'class prep' and 'drinks with friends' and essentially allergic to picking up the phone. It will come as no surprise that he broke up with me. Well, he didn't technically break up *with* me. He just broke away from the situation and left without any real explanation.

Can you even say you've been in your twenties if you haven't had a series of boyfriends who were totally wrong for you? Heartbroken and pitiful, the last thing I wanted to do was go back to teaching, so I took a job doing telesales for Torwood Lounge in Ramsgate. This involved sitting at a desk all day and ringing people to see if they wanted to hire the venue. My other responsibilities included setting the tables for weddings. Every time I tried to make a table look presentable, I kept thinking, *Why me?* I'm the least design-minded person ever. Whenever I tried to get creative with a centrepiece or fold a napkin in a special way, it wound up looking more like the scene of a feral cat fight. Thankfully, I didn't have to endure this job much longer because the owner cornered me in the walk-in freezer and started coming onto me. I quit on the spot and never went back.

One of the many life rules I live by is: don't ever work for someone who makes you feel uncomfortable ... even if it means being jobless, approaching thirty and living at home with your parents.

Sounding like I was coming down with something, Mum eventually had to drag me to the doctor who gave me the fantastic diagnosis of pneumonitis. At first I thought I contracted it on the plane, but it was more likely from my constant smoking and lack of exercise.

For weeks I used what little energy I had to move my body from bed to our back porch to sit in the sun. No, I didn't stop smoking. I just prayed that a bit of vitamin D would help. Or at least give me tanned skin to hide the circles under my eyes and weight around my face. This was arguably one of the lowest moments of my life, made only lower by a package I received in the mail from Des soon after. When I opened it, I found a beautiful wooden jewellery box lined with velvet. Inside the box, a note read:

Dear Lynne,

I really enjoyed our time together, but I've fallen in love with a girl named Anne Marie. I hope you're still happy with Peter and are glad to be home. Thank you for the memories.

Love,

Des

Ouch. Salt in the wound.

CHAPTER 7
Back in the Game

Here's the thing – I really wasn't that upset about Des *or* Peter. Deep down I knew that Des was just a holiday fling and Peter was simply eye candy. (Seriously, the guy was so hot.) My low stemmed from feeling rejected, which I think most people can relate to. I think most people will also relate when I say that there's nothing a little indulgent self-pity can't fix. (TV, comfort food, wine – rinse and repeat.)

By January 1979, I was on the mend and back at the Q Theatre to perform in the kids' production, *Old King Cole*. Now *this* was how I liked interacting with the youth of Australia! With my face dotted with freckles and my hair divided into pigtails and adorned with yarn, I proudly bounced around the stage as Princess Daphne Cole and may or may not have canoodled backstage with Alan, who was playing Twoo. Every bit as playful as his character, Alan gave me the church giggles at the most inopportune moments. Our relationship turned romantic at the cast party, but abruptly ended when I found out he'd fallen for an up-and-coming actress who would go on to be very successful and internationally famous. (I'd tell you who, but then I'd have to kill you.) I was sad about this, but eventually became kind of excited that said superstar and I had shared the same mouth. I also firmly believed that there are plenty more leading men in the sea! #ontothenext

Speaking of famous actors, Judy Davis also performed at the Q. Yes, the incredibly talented Judy Davis from *Ratched*, *The Dressmaker*, *Husbands and Wives* and countless other award-worthy films, plays and television series. While she wasn't someone who would smoke dope with us in between rehearsals or make inappropriate jokes about bowel movements, our paths did cross when she was cast as Kati in *The Good Soldier Švejk*.

Judy had just starred in *My Brilliant Career* and both she and the film were nominated for a long list of awards. Knowing that she may need to jet off to Cannes, the US or the UK at any point,

I was cast as her understudy. During rehearsals, I couldn't help but notice how focused and emotionally invested she was in her role. I've always considered myself professional, but those NIDA (National Institute of Dramatic Art) grads were on a whole other level. While the proof is clearly in the pudding (the pudding being scores of BAFTA, Emmy and Academy awards and the fact that Judy did indeed need me to fill in for her so she could continue on her path to stardom) I liked to approach performing a little differently.

Put simply: I wanted to have fun.

With Judy off collecting gongs and teeing up projects with people like Woody Allen, I took the character of Kati to the stage and concentrated on earning as much money as possible. I'd recently moved into a little funky house in St Mary's in Sydney's west with John White and Fiona Press, two friends from the Q. Even though my theatre work was growing more and more consistent, I started doing relief teaching on the side so that I had some savings to fall back on. (Can you tell I'm an accountant's daughter?)

Back in the day, there were only three (very long) school terms. In most cases, the Year 6s had completed their exams and finished all of the work required to move on to high school by the end of the second term. This meant the third term was essentially teachers just babysitting thirty-five prepubescent kids whose personalities could only be described as vile, revolting and/or unmotivated.

As a result, the full-time teachers often chose to take their holidays or long service leave during third term, which meant as a relief teacher I was in for a very hard slog. To make matters worse, the school I worked at had 'streamed' classes. This meant the less academically inclined kids were in C or D class, the average kids in B and the so-called 'gifted' kids in A class. Can you guess what I got? A combination of C and D class consisting of – wait for it – forty-three students. As if the sheer number of bodies in one room wasn't enough to make you want to run for the hills, there were several kids with learning disabilities and autism.

As someone with very little teaching experience, it breaks my heart and seems wildly unfair that those kids got me as a teacher. Not that I wasn't loving and kind, I just didn't have enough support or experience to know how to give one on one attention or offer alternative learning solutions. One of my students, Mark, could read and recall everything from the twenty books he consumed every day, but was as useless as tits on a bull when it came to maths. In any event, his mother wrote me the kindest letter saying how much he loved being in my class. While I like to think letting him read until the cows came home was what endeared me to him, it was more likely the fact that I was a woman and he hated men. The previous year he'd bashed a male teacher over the head with a metal folding chair. Regardless, Mark was obviously my favourite.

If 1978 had been the lowest of lows, 1979 was definitely the highest of highs. At long last I realised that I could never leave the stage for an extended period of time again. On top of working professionally at the Q, I was doing a part-time drama course two nights a week with all-day Saturday rehearsals. I studied tap dancing, Irish dancing and even did some pointe work. Eventually I had such consistent employment that I found myself instinctively putting on an extra croaky voice in the mornings if the phone rang before 8 a.m. I knew it was most likely the school needing a substitute teacher.

'Hello?' I'd answer sounding like Tom Waits and Kim Carnes' love child.

'Hi Lynne? It's Mrs Kearns calling from York Road Public School. Just wondering if you're free to teach a Year 6 class today?'

Cue: repulsive cough. 'I'm so sorry, but I'm a bit crook today.'

This type of performance went on for months. Finally, I'd just pick the receiver up and drop it right back down. The truth was, I was living and breathing the theatre and really only wanted to be near other people who felt the same way. Fiona Press was perfect because she was adamant about studying at NIDA. It took her three auditions over three years – probably because she was a teenager when she first tried and they wanted people with more life experience – but she eventually got in and became a highly respected and wonderfully talented actress.

Despite having more front than Myer, I never wanted to apply for NIDA because I didn't think I could handle the rejection. For much of my adult life, I felt like a performer, not an actor. Only later did I feel like I grew into my acting shoes.

My other housemate, John White, and I always enjoyed a cheeky spliff together. Together, we'd all get stoned, listen to 'Solid Rock' by Goanna and discuss plays, music and other actors. Doreen, the Q's fearless leader, was always so supportive of us but she was nothing if not a realist. I recall her telling me, 'Darling, you're very good, but you need to lose that *awful* Australian accent.' I also recall her walking in on us one day, sniffing the air and yelling, 'Pot!' before slamming the door, which obviously made us wet ourselves with laughter.

Another champion around this time was the director, Kevin Jackson. Kevin told me, 'You'll make it as an actor because you're not afraid to be ugly.' While some people might cock their head and think, *Wow, what a dick*, I didn't. Because he wasn't. I knew what he meant. He recognised that my acting wasn't dependent on how I looked. (Just flip to the photo section if you need further proof.)

Truthfully, I didn't really know what I was doing. I had very little technical nous when it came to the fundamentals of drama, but I was always happy to jump in boots and all. To this day, I'm still a bit like this. Even on *Home and Away*, if I have to do something extreme, I always go huge because it's much easier to let a director reel me back in. Some of the young actors are so minimalist. This is all well and good until they realise they're playing a character on a soap opera, which means they need to be able to do drunk, drug-addled, murderous rage, torrid affair or suffering from hypothermia and starvation while draped down a mineshaft full of funnel webs. Frequently all at once. Not being afraid to be ugly essentially means not being afraid to fail. That's what Kevin Jackson taught me.

Doreen and Kevin's encouragement led me to play Rosalind in *As You Like It*, Maria in *Twelfth Night*, Miss Damina in *Don't Just Lie There, Say Something* and eventually Lust in *Paradise Regained*. This show was particularly memorable because we had a new stage manager, whom I shall call Pipe Man. He made backstage feel more like Nazi Germany due to his stiff posture, authoritative tone and unwillingness to tolerate excuses from anyone about their tardiness. Oh and he smoked a pipe.

As a student of NIDA, Pipe Man took his management

position very seriously while at work, but outside of work I discovered a surprisingly fun and very attractive side. Together we'd zoom around on his motorbike, go to shows and spend afternoons with our legs entwined in bed. We were actually spending so much time together that I realised there wasn't a way to hide my laxative addiction. Knowing deep down that it was terrible for my body and mortified at the thought of Pipe Man discovering my crutch, I went cold turkey. I haven't touched one since.

In a flash, twelve months passed and we found ourselves discussing serious matters. Like children.

'We better get married if we're going to have kids together,' he said.

So we did.

I married Pipe Man in 1981 and had a reception at Victoria House in Bexley. Our families and friends from the Q, college and even high school attended. We stayed in a motel in Blakehurst on our wedding night before flying to Tasmania for our honeymoon. As much as I would love to report that we did nothing but have day sex and sightsee, I spent most of the time carsick from traipsing around in our campervan.

Once we got home, my parents were desperate for us to come by theirs to open our wedding gifts. My uncles and aunties had given us a handsome cheque, while an actor friend gave us a hookah. I'll never forget the curious looks on my parents' faces as I tried to explain it was something you smoked tobacco out of. The next gift was from my high school friend Tom. I was terrified of opening it because from my light handling of the hard container – and knowing Tom – I was convinced it was an ounce of dope. With sweat trickling down my back, I unwrapped the gift and have never been so relieved to see two beautiful pens. I excused myself to go to the loo because I had just about shat myself. But the best wedding gift we received was an invitation to live in a house that Dad had recently bought in Hazelbrook in the Blue Mountains. (At mate's rates.)

While I spent most of my time either acting, taking acting classes or hanging out with my acting friends, Pipe Man was either doing work as a stage manager or driving taxis. But just six months in I couldn't help feeling a sense of dread every time I had to drive up the mountains to our home. Something was wrong, but I couldn't put my finger on it. Maybe it was personality differences or incompatibility of our immune systems, but after a year I didn't want him to touch me. I tried to convince myself that it was just a phase. Or maybe all marriages were like this and I was just imagining conflict. I was at a loss. I'd always envisioned marriage and a happily ever after ... but this was marriage and a 'Oh God, I don't want to go home'.

And to be honest – I didn't go home much. I often found

myself crashing with friends, Jane and Felix. They had a terrible relationship. Felix was a raging alcoholic and emotionally and verbally abusive. Eventually it became glaringly obvious that I needed to do something about Pipe Man if I preferred being in the firing line of a toxic relationship rather than in his presence.

On the last day of winter in 1982, I moved out of our marital home and moved in with Jane and Felix. I had asked Pipe Man to meet me for dinner in Penrith a few weeks earlier. I could tell he knew something was wrong, but what broke me was how devastated and confused he looked when I said I wanted us to separate. Apparently he thought I just wanted a break. Yes, I did. But forever.

It's awful being this direct, but when it comes to ripping a Band-Aid off a relationship that simply can't be held together and needs to bleed out, you have to say things like, 'I don't love you and I cannot live a lie. You take all the wedding gifts and furniture. I'll move out.'

When we finished eating, he went home to Hazelbrook.

I called Dad, who proceeded to tell me he and Mum never thought our relationship would last. In my head I kept thinking, *Gee, that information would have been nice two years ago*, but let's be honest – I probably wouldn't have listened.

Dad assured me he'd help me undo our marriage and that he did. He let Pipe Man stay in the Hazelbrook house, but went up to get my stuff. Eventually, Pipe Man moved to Queensland. I haven't seen him since that dinner in Penrith and he seemed to lose contact with everybody. I heard whispers that he thought I'd been having an affair with John Scott, which was not true.

Although it didn't look great when I started dating John about a year later.

After living with Jane and Felix for a few months, I moved in with the aforementioned John Scott and John White of St Mary's days. I consciously took things quite slowly with John and was candid about where my priorities lay: in the theatre. Agreeable and patient, we enjoyed each other's company and formed a nice bond. As well as acting, John played the bodhran in an Irish folk band so most Friday nights I'd accompany him to a woolshed bush dance out woop woop somewhere.

In 1983, we went up to visit my parents in Brisbane because Dad had recently taken a job there working with Rothwells merchant bank's now infamous Laurie Connell. Dad, who was as honest as the day is long, quickly learnt that Laurie was not. After witnessing some highly illegal activities he wrote Laurie a letter outlining who was involved, explicitly expressing that he was *not* happy about it, and that he wanted to resign. Laurie pleaded with him to stay and fix it. Even though he relented, Dad wisely kept a copy of the letter in his safe in anticipation of the police knocking on his door one day ... which of course they did! But just as Dad was gearing up to be a witness in the case, Laurie died in his sleep from a heart attack.

But before this real life *Peaky Blinders* behaviour went down, John and I were enjoying our holiday in the sunshine state and checking out his old stomping ground, La Boite Theatre. In the lobby, I perused the noticeboard and saw an advertisement for the Murray River Performing Group's (MRPG) upcoming auditions in Sydney. I knew about them because they were home to the Flying Fruit Fly Circus and were expanding into theatre with shows like *Crystal Dewdrops* and *Back to Dean Street*.

Feeling motivated and antsy for a change of scenery, I went back to Sydney and auditioned for the MRPG's David Ogilvy, Lynda Gibson (also known as Gibbo) and some other intimidating faces. Along with Johnny Walker and Rosie John, I was offered a spot and moved down to Albury–Wodonga at the start of 1984.

Leaving the Q felt a little like leaving high school: equal parts earth-shattering and monumental. It was the sort of departure where you want to hug everyone extra-long and make promises to stay in touch forever (and sometimes you do), but you're also eager to see what else is out there. Sometimes in life, even when everything seems to be going right, it's okay to make a decision to move on, even if you're not one hundred per cent sure it's the right thing to do.

While John Scott and I were still together, it was clear he wasn't happy about me packing up and making a new life in Albury. He came to visit a few times, but we drifted apart, which was fine with me because I was absolutely loving my new adventure. For starters, I was living with one of my fellow actor recruits, Rosie, on George Street near the Star Hotel. This was a prime spot because it was within walking distance of both the theatre and a servo that sold fantastic snacks for when we had the munchies.

A reader of tarot cards, Rosie and I spent much of our downtime learning about my past, present and future. At every reading, she would tell me I'd never have money worries and that the great love of my life was just around the corner. We did this weekly and there was never any deviation.

As someone who was raised Anglican (but had obviously strayed *very* far from the church's standard of living), I quietly wondered if what Rosie and I were doing was a little bit pagan. I wasn't concerned enough to not do it, just aware that maybe it's not something my old minister would have approved of. Funny how all the pot smoking, casual sex and boundary-pushing scripts never seemed to give me pause though. Also funny how I didn't blink twice when I found myself sort of dating an inmate at Beechworth Correctional Centre.

One of the fun parts of working at the MRPG was getting to take shows on the road or, in this particular instance, to a prison. As you'll have guessed by now I love a chat, so prison shows really suited me because the audience was desperate for outside energy and interaction. After finishing a performance of *Bleedin' Butterflies*, I had the pleasure of meeting an inmate named Jim, who was a talented potter. While admiring his collection of ceramic bowls, I casually asked him what he was in for.

'Drugs.'

Not surprised, I responded, 'Ridiculous, eh? They really need to decriminalise dope.'

Jim added, 'I also stabbed a cop.'

Oh. This information made me slightly apprehensive about continuing our conversation, but the thing was, Jim was kind of cute, very into me and offering me loads of handmade pottery.

Casually dating/not really dating a guy in prison has its pros and cons. (See what I did there?) After a few assignations with Jim, I understood why women fall for men on death row. Because the inmates have so much time and no real responsibilities, their love letters are lengthy, meet-ups steamy and prison gifts extremely thoughtful. You're basically the sole focus of their life. Don't worry, I wasn't thinking about marrying Jim. I just thought he was nice and enjoyed our chats in the yard.

Nevertheless, it didn't take me long to realise I'm the wrong kind of jail girlfriend … you see, I ask too many questions.

'What's that guy in for?' I asked of a fellow inmate one afternoon while sitting on a plastic picnic table and fondling a freshly kilned biscuit jar.

Jim shook his head. 'Oh, that dude's bad. He killed his wife with an axe.'

It was at this moment that I became aware that I was in the yard of a jail, fraternising with 'Jim the Crim' while an axe murderer was just metres away.

I decided it was time to go.

With my penitentiary dating days behind me, I dove back into my MRPG life and we started writing and rehearsing an off-colour Christmas comedy revue called *Immaculate Deception*. The show was cabaret meets college revue meets *The Bitches* meets *A Christmas Carol*. We'd get quite political, personal and riff on people like Bob Hawke (who was obviously the Messiah) and Robert Trimboli (you know, the gangster from Griffith who fled to Ireland, got cancer and died).

The biggest difference between the Q and the MRPG is that while we would be performing one show, we'd often be writing the next. We also had a very attractive pianist named Paul McWaters, who made me say out loud in the most unladylike way, 'I've got to get me one of those!' when I spotted him during a rehearsal at the Galah Bar. Who was this guy? Was he single? Did he mingle? Where did he learn to play like that?

Unlike my willingness to make the first move with Jim the Crim, I found myself nervous whenever Paul was in the room and unsure how to let my arms hang. Since I love naps as much as I love snacks, after a big morning of rehearsals one day I went into the music room during my lunch break to have a little lie down. I was startled to see Paul sitting perfectly still at his keyboard with his eyes closed. While I had met him briefly, I really didn't know him well enough to ask if he was currently high on heroin or having a diabetic episode. He sensed my presence, opened his eyes and miraculously, I came up with a third possible excuse.

'Are you ... meditating?' I asked.

I could tell from the look on his face that he was impressed that I knew what meditation was. You need to remember that in the early 1980s, we didn't have Instagram feeds, Facebook groups and podcast ads telling us to download mindfulness apps and to meditate for at least ten minutes a day. We were too busy chain-smoking fags and drinking Tab for that. Once Paul affirmed that he was indeed meditating, I discovered that he was from the area, very into music and had recently ended a five-year engagement. It was quite obvious that if Paul was going to enter a new relationship, things would need to move at a glacial pace.

I respected this and backed off ... for a few days.

My friend Sally-Anne Upton (aka Sal) could see that Paul and I had chemistry and kept encouraging me to invite him over for dinner. Since I didn't want him to feel pressured or like we were on a date, I made Sal come too. Why I felt game enough to prepare food intended to be eaten by humans, I'll never know. It was probably just my desire to impress Paul. Regardless, I laboured over beef burgundy and couldn't wait to show him what a domestic goddess I was. Talented on and off the stage. What a catch! #winkyface

Halfway through our meal, I couldn't help noticing just how buzzed and chatty Paul seemed to be. I was actually feeling quite dizzy too. Turns out it's easy to get shit-faced when your beef burgundy contains no less than a litre of red wine and hasn't been cooked long enough. By dessert, Paul and I had both let our inhibitions go and were all over each other. Sal whispered to me that she felt like a gooseberry and was going to leave. Much to my delight, Paul stayed.

And stayed and stayed and stayed.

And he still hasn't gone home.

ACTING UP

I don't think we came up for air for about a year. Truly the definition of 'besotted', I moved out of the home I was sharing with Rosie and in with Paul and another couple in Mayfair Drive, Wodonga. While yes, I was madly in love with Paul and wanted to live with him, I was also anxious to get out of my house because you didn't even need white witch powers to pick up its odd vibe. I'm not one to believe in the boogieman, but we both agreed that the house had bad juju.

Unfortunately, Paul's house was equally uncomfortable because the couple we lived with were *very* expressive in the bedroom. I'm talking next level loud. While trying to fall asleep at night, I'd be startled awake by an actual 'Yee-haw!' accompanied by the beat of a headboard banging against the wall. To be honest, I was shocked that one of their heads never came flying through the gyprock.

Paul and I soon moved into a cute 1940s-era cottage on Electra Street in East Albury. Instead of moans, groans and porn-worthy sex noises, we now enjoyed the sweet chirps from the birdlife that flocked to our large garden. I know it's annoying when someone describes their relationship as one big honeymoon, but the first decade with Paul really was. We lived together, played together and worked together.

One of our most enjoyable performances was a play called *Around the Bend*, based on the real-life experience of journalists John Hindle, John Hepworth and Patrick Amer, who rafted down the Murray River from Albury–Wodonga to Lake Alexandrina. John Walker played Hindle, I played Hepworth, Gibbo played Amer and Rosie played the Little Helmsman. Together, we embraced the rowdy and alcoholic traits of these famous and hilarious journos.

Around the Bend was such a hit we ended up doing it a second time and took the show on the road, visiting places like Corowa, Echuca, Renmark, Robinvale and a town called Berri. (Not to be confused with the NSW south coast Berry you're probably thinking of.) By the time we got to Renmark, the weather was starting to warm up, so we decided to stop and have lunch on the banks of the Murray River. After months of rugging up, it was so nice to feel the warm sun on our skin as we unwrapped our sandwiches and cracked our cans of soft drink.

Just as I was about to deep throat a chicken schnitzel burger, I found myself discombobulated. Everything was dark. A sharp pain was piercing both my eye and my neck. Everything smelled … fishy. That's when I realised that I was the one being deep throated … by a pelican! After coming to the conclusion that I'd need to let go of my burger and let it drop into the depths of this devil pelican's guts, I worked on an escape plan. By the grace of God, Paul chucked a can at it and rescued me. Expecting to be greeted by an ambo, I only saw the laughing faces and pee-stained pants of my cast mates. As much as I would love to agree that pelicans are one of Australia's most majestic bird species, I'm not going to lie … seeing that pelican get shot at the end of *Storm Boy* actually gave me the peace and closure I needed after my attack. (Sorry to all of my animal-loving friends. I promise that no pelicans were harmed in the production of this book.)

When I wasn't being attacked by wildlife, loving Paul or doing something classed as 'serious theatre', I was helping develop an MRPG comedy troupe called *The Sensational Spangles* alongside Sal, Johnny Walker, Al Mullins, David Ogilvy and you guessed it, Paul. The premise of our troupe was to be idiots and sing 1960s songs. Pretty groundbreaking stuff if you ask me. Even though the *Spangles* were selling out shows and receiving good reviews, certain people at the government-funded MRPG hated us, which made our mandatory meetings unbearable.

Meetings to me are right up there with filling out forms. At these meetings, it was obvious that a couple of the artistic directors wanted the MRPG to be synonymous with 'serious' and 'dramatic'. They didn't want *anything* commercial. Being part of a conglomerate also meant needing to cover a wide range of genres, not just comedy. While I loved that they wanted to produce theatre that was politically charged, boundary pushing and indeed, worthy of awards, the fact of the matter is a show about the desalination of the Murray, although highly commendable (and politically correct), is hardly a knees-up night out. Especially when you live in a rural town. Sometimes you just need to sell some damn tickets.

The Sensational Spangles were deemed too 'commercial and mindless' for these guys. Eventually, we got to a point of contention where the troupe knew we weren't going to find common ground. At our last meeting we were left with these words ringing in our ears, '*The Sensational Spangles* are artistically unsound, financially unviable and philosophically f*cked!'

It was actually quite poetic.

On that note, Paul, the rest of the actors and I decided to take our act and end our tenure with the MRPG. We created a production company called Funny Business in 1986 and spent the next two years kicking some major goals. Looking back, I'm so impressed that we were able to survive without any government grants or arts subsidies. Remember, this was during a recession and Australia had one of the strictest budgets of all time. I think what made us viable was that unlike community theatre that works hard on one show, performs it for a few weeks and then shelves it, our goal with Funny Business was to create acts that could continue to grow and evolve: be evergreen in a sense. This helped keep our costs low and energy levels high.

As well as the *Spangles*, we did performances called *Don't Rock The Boat*, *Red Herrings* and *Sanity Clauses*. People loved us and it was the support of our venues and audiences that helped us take a *Spangles* show down to Melbourne to do a four-week stint at Le Joke comedy club. I was in absolute heaven. In my eyes, Melbourne was a comedian's mecca and oh how I wanted to make my pilgrimage. After nearly three years, Funny Business came to its own natural conclusion after many of us started gravitating away from Albury–Wodonga.

After having such a great time in Melbourne, Paul and I started talking about moving south. He had grown up in Albury–Wodonga and was open for a change. A few of our other actor friends like Gibbo and Scotty had already shifted to Melbourne. In 1988 we took the plunge and along with David Ogilvy moved into a charming worker's cottage in Burnley, close to Richmond.

While you might think David was our third wheel, there was actually a fourth in the home, a gargantuan Great Dane who answered to Roxy. We often felt sad for Roxy because our tiny backyard must have been like hovering over a puppy pad to her. A few months in, we made the decision to send her to Albury where Jeff (our techie '*Spangle*') and his wife and kids were living on a nice big property. Since no good deed goes unpunished, she wasn't there for very long before she ate a box of snail killer and died. (I'd like to apologise for that depressing dog story, but remember – keep your poisons up high! Especially if you own a dumb but cute Great Dane.)

While moving to Melbourne was proving to be a very good decision, we did go back to Albury for one last hurrah on New Year's Eve 1988. Somehow, *The Sensational Spangles* had managed to attract 5500 people to a show at Mungabareena Reserve on the banks of the Murray. Unlike the intimate cubby-house theatres we were used to, this stage was huge, the crowds reminiscent of Woodstock and the chants for us to come onstage absolutely thundering. Or was it *actual* thunder?

As showtime approached, we had all been anxiously watching a storm on the horizon. Fearing that we'd be rocking and rolling in mud and at risk of being struck by lightning, at the last second, this very angry storm thankfully made a sharp turn to the right and granted us clear skies.

It was to be the last time we performed as *The Sensational Spangles*.

John, Sal, David, Al, Paul and I often talk about how successful a *Spangles Revisited* show would be. We're totally up for it ... as long as fans don't mind watching us dance with Zimmer frames and walking sticks. I actually think it would do well because to this day, despite having played Irene on *Home and Away* for nearly thirty years and having not done the *Spangles* for *over* thirty years, I still can't walk down the streets of Albury–Wodonga without someone yelling out of a car, 'Hey, Stella!' We're all still around with the exception of Jeff Larson, our technical manager, who sadly passed away a few years ago. RIP Jeff.

CHAPTER 8
Thirty-Something

Before Paul and I fell madly in love, spent four years working on shows together and made the decision to move to Melbourne, he had planned to go overseas in an effort to shake off his previous five-year engagement. As he likes to say, he spent one year engaged, four years trying to get out of it and was in need of some distance between him and that period of his life. But, as you recall, I won his heart with my undercooked beef burgundy at the end of 1984, causing him to stick around and shelve his plans for a grand tour. Because I knew just how much fun and how formative travel is, I felt guilty about what had happened, which is why when he suggested a six-week overseas trip at the end of 1988 I was a hard yes!

Even though we felt the same amount of love, comfort and respect we'd shown each other in the early butterfly stages of our courtship, part of me wondered how we'd fare while travelling. It's no secret that some people suck to travel with. From projecting airport check-in anxiety on you to making an awkward and judgemental comment about a country's culture, you just never know if one small action or word is going to snowball into a fit of passive-aggressive rage that is now triggered by them simply squeezing the toothpaste from the middle of the tube. Confident that Paul was practically perfect in every way, I pushed that small worry to the side and excitedly started planning our trip.

A self-confessed Anglophile, I simply cannot get enough of all things English. I love the history, the architecture, the art, the tea and the Royal Family. Another argument I had for going to England was that Paul had never been there. Not a fan of the UK's reputation for blisteringly cold winters (and springs, summers and autumns), Paul wanted to go somewhere warmer. Ultimately we compromised and decided that as well as the UK, we'd go to Greece, and then Israel on the way home, as Paul's sister had just been there and raved about it.

We excitedly booked our tickets aboard the ever-affordable Olympic Airlines, which meant two stopovers – one in Singapore and one in Athens. What happened next can only be described as the ultimate relationship test. The leg from Melbourne to Singapore was to be as expected: overcrowded, filled with pure sodium disguised as food, and the type of seat spacing that makes you contort to the shape of a pretzel. Grateful to land safely, we were annoyed to hear that our flight to Athens was delayed … by eight hours. As much as I wish I could say that Paul and I spent that time wandering through the famous Changi Airport butterfly garden or catching a blockbuster in Terminal 2, neither of those things existed yet so we mostly just sat around chain-smoking.

Finally back on board and soaring through the sky, we snuggled into each other and tried to sleep. Before having the chance to reach anything close to a REM cycle, we were jolted awake and told the plane was running out of fuel and would need to make an emergency landing.

In Dubai.

This was ever so slightly terrifying.

I'm not a nervous flyer, but when someone tells me we're going to run out of fuel 36,000 feet in the air, I get uneasy. Paul was cool and collected and just the right amount of calm I needed.

My fellow passengers on the other hand were losing their minds.

You see, this was during the first Intifada and many Jewish people chose to fly with Olympic Airlines because they didn't make stops in the Middle East. Worried that upon landing to refuel their passports would be inspected and they would be found to be Israeli, they audibly expressed their fear of being hauled off never to be seen or heard from again.

As we touched down in Dubai, I understood their fear. Men with black masks and machine guns were everywhere, which was incredibly intimidating. Thankfully, we didn't need to disembark and we refuelled in a timely manner. With the plane's nose pointed to the sky once again, our sense of relief to be on our way was shattered by an almighty crashing sound.

I whipped my head towards Paul. *What now?* 'Did we just lose a wing?' I gasped.

Paul, the ever sensible one, surveyed the plane and realised what had happened. 'The breakfast trays just went flying out of the galley. The flight attendant mustn't have latched them down.'

'The *hot* breakfast?' I asked, acting like losing my next meal was worse than losing a wing.

But I wasn't alone. The only thing louder than the trays going flying was the complaints spewing forth from our fellow passengers at our poor flight attendant. The poor thing couldn't have been more than twenty-two. As paying customers, the other passengers were extremely pissed to learn that the few hot breakfast trays that did survive were given to the returning crew members. Since verbal complaints weren't enough, a few men proceeded to have an actual punch up.

Even though I was also peeved about not getting to eat the science experiment they call airplane food, I tried to rationalise my disappointment by remembering that the people flying airplanes and essentially holding every passenger's life in their hands should be well fed and nowhere near 'hangry'.

While I would love to say that this travel day from hell ended there, it didn't. Once we landed in Athens, the stampede of Italian and Greek people who missed their flights because of the unscheduled fuel stop didn't care who or what they took down while trying to get to the ticketing counter. As a glass barrier broke between the airline representatives and the rabid crowd, young employees literally ran away crying. For the next hour, the company refused to serve anyone because they were so scared.

Rightly so.

As order was regained, Paul and I decided to bail on Olympic (we both knew when it was time to leave a bad relationship) and rebook our flight to London with Swiss Air. As planned, we left the airport to spend one night in the Greek capital.

I am certain that Athens is a marvellous city full of kind

people, extraordinary history, delicious food and streets begging to be explored, but for the short amount of time I was there, my only real memory was walking in a zombie-like trance past shops with X-rated magazines hung up in the windows. Much to the appreciation of my innocent eyes, the pink bits had been blacked out.

It could have been our extreme fatigue, lack of food or the dangerously high levels of cortisol coursing through our bodies, but we decided we didn't want to come back to Greece after Israel.

Our Swiss Air flight to London via Geneva the next day was uneventful. Actually, there was one event my snack-loving self will never forget: due to a shortage of food in economy, Paul and I were served fillet steak and lobster from business class!

Once safely in London we checked into a nice bed and breakfast in Bayswater, which, unlike the accommodation on my first trip to London, was *not* staffed by cockroaches (or no-pants Lindsay). It's so interesting to go back to a city you had previously visited in your youth. Seeing London as a 35-year-old and in a relationship allowed me to take in so much more of the city, as well as England's vast and green countryside. I also wasn't stoned the whole time. We caught a bus down to Devon, wandered around Cornwall and splurged on romantic dinners in ritzy London suburbs like Putney, Fulham and Chelsea. After having to subsist on boiled eggs, tomato soup and Vegemite on toast back in the 1970s, indulging in world-class English, French and Italian cuisine was a real treat.

We also bought tickets to see Rowan Atkinson (Mr Bean!) and Timothy West in *The Sneeze* at the Aldwych Theatre. Translated and adapted by Michael Frayn, *The Sneeze* consists of seven short Anton Chekhov plays. The show was bloody fantastic, but unfortunately, my knees were not fantastic – only bloody. While running from the bus to the theatre I tripped, became airborne and face planted, which caused me to make less than graceful contact with the footpath. My black stockings were now one with my kneecaps, my hands scraped raw and my chin sanded back to a nice ruby red. People always tell me they envy my long thin legs, but I'm the first to say that they're not very good at keeping me upright!

Just as my knee scabs allowed for a full range of motion, our time in the UK came to an end and we took off for Tel Aviv, Israel. At the time, the Israeli–Palestinian conflict was making headlines because a fifteen-year-old Israeli girl was shot and killed in the West Bank. The news made quite a few people, my parents included, comment that it was an odd thing to holiday in a war zone. In our minds, the actual warfare seemed to be happening in Lebanon and the occurrences of suicide bombers had yet to escalate. We felt like Israel's dependence on tourism would help keep us safe. (And of course our journey with Olympic Airlines from Melbourne to Athens made a war zone look good.)

Aside from a few skip bins being pushed over haphazardly on the street and teens throwing rocks at passing police and army Jeeps, Israel did make us feel safe and welcome. Over the next couple of weeks, we floated in the Dead Sea (thank God my footpath scabs were fully healed), took a boat ride on the Sea of Galilee (which is actually a lake), and hiked to the top of the eerie Masada in the Judean Desert (where I rediscovered my fear of heights). We also hopped on a bus tour that took us to Jerusalem where we saw things like the fourteen Stations of the Cross, the Dome of the Rock and of course a slew of street-smart child-hecklers who wouldn't let us pass without giving them a shekel.

'Come on, American. Please, just one shekel!' they'd beg in unison.

'First of all, I'm not American. I'm Australian …' But before I could finish part two of my 'I don't want to give you a shekel' speech, their eyes grew wide and they erupted in excitement.

'Australian? It's Linda Kozlowski! It's Linda Kozlowski! *Two shekels!* Dundee can give us more!'

While the Dundee references were wearing on me, I was admittedly flattered that my new short dirty-blonde hairdo meant people were mistaking me for the iconic Linda Kozlowski. Grateful for the compliment, I tossed the kids two shekels and we went on our way.

I don't know if Paul and I were the only tourists in Tel Aviv but we stood out like a koala in Coles. I felt like a street-style queen because the women there, who clearly had big money and loved anything to do with western style and culture, assumed I was from America. I take full credit for the tartan trend making it to the Middle East. For most of the trip I wore a mini drop-waist long-sleeve tartan dress with a Peter Pan collar. Israeli women dripping with gold didn't even try to hide the fact that they were staring me up and down when I'd be browsing in a shop. (You're welcome, Sussan.)

One of the most memorable places we visited was the Wailing Wall. At the risk of sounding altruistic, I wrote a note praying for peace and placed it in a crack on the women's side. (That almost sounds rude.) I know conflict resolution takes time, but my heart breaks thinking about the current situation in Israel three decades later. When we ventured to the Negev Desert to see the remnants of the Six Day War, we got out of our car to look at one of the blown-up Elephant tanks that had been left as a memorial. That's when we heard, 'Oi! Mate!' Straight away we knew we were being beckoned by Aussies. The only other tourists on our little Tour de War Zone were another couple from Melbourne. After some pleasant exchanges about where we had been as well as a small bonding session over how many times we'd been asked about *Crocodile Dundee*, we said our goodbyes.

One of the things I love most about Australians is how we've always loved to travel. (I also love that we'll throw a going away party even if you're only gone for six weeks.)

Our final adventure in Israel involved driving to Bethlehem. Even though you'd think driving around Israel's famously barren countryside would have been a walk in the park compared to navigating Sydney's frenzied maze of a roadway system, we managed to get so lost. At one point we were staring down a stretch of road that had a sign with a donkey. After a light debate about if the sign meant 'donkeys only' or 'watch out for donkeys', we decided to keep going. While this didn't feel like the most convenient route to Bethlehem, we thought, *This just must be how roads are here.*

Evidently, no.

Two heavily armed, burly Palestinians appeared out of nowhere and signalled for us to stop. When they stepped up to our rolled down window, I saw them eyeing our number plate, which featured Hebrew letters.

'*Ivrit?*' they asked. (Which means 'Hebrew?')

I cleared my throat and answered, 'Aussie!' (Let's be honest – there's English and then there's Aussie.)

Both man mountains suddenly looked warm and friendly as huge smiles came across their faces.

'Ah! Dundee!' (Again.)

After a bit of role-playing of *'That's* not a knife!' an Israeli military Jeep pulled up and we learnt that the road we were on was very much a road just for donkeys (and military). We also learnt that it led in the direction of the West Bank, not Bethlehem. We farewelled our new Palestinian friends and were escorted to Bethlehem by the Israeli military jeep.

Bethlehem was my favourite place in Israel because I was becoming increasingly curious about my birthright as a Christian. (Interesting fact: although I was raised Anglican and consider myself Anglican today, Paul recently did genealogy work on my family. We discovered that my maternal great-grandfather was Jewish. After doing genetic testing, it was confirmed I have about forty per cent Western European Jew in me. *Mazel tov!*)

Our first stop was at the Church of the Nativity, which is built over the cave where Jesus was born in Manger Square. (I don't know why I find the fact that they named this spot 'Manger Square' so funny. To this day I keep wondering that if Jesus had been crucified on Market Street in Sydney, would they have named it Crucifixion Centrepoint?)

We met a lovely French–Palestinian Christian man, Raymonde, who asked if he could be our tour guide for a small fee. He showed us around and had a wealth of knowledge about the birthplace of Jesus Christ. The most surprising thing about visiting the Church of the Nativity was the constant bickering between the original Eastern Christian bodies about the literal location of Jesus Christ's birthplace. I kid you not, in an area containing four quadrants no bigger than four square metres, they would yell things like, 'This is where Jesus was born! No this was! No *this* was!' and 'Christmas Day is in January! Not December!' and 'That's not where Calvary was!'

The only fact that everyone agreed on was where the Last Supper was held. Raymonde also told us how they would pilfer candles and other relics from each other's quadrants. While I may have mostly been playing spin the bottle in Sunday School, I'm pretty sure 'Don't argue over silly things' is Religion 101, right? I was and still am under the impression that as long as you're not worshipping a shrub and I'm not worshipping a quokka, we can put our differences (like where Mary's amniotic fluid may have splashed) aside.

As the sun began to set, Raymonde told us we should move our car to the police station parking lot to avoid it being nicked. Then he invited us for dinner. That night we shared a delicious meal at Raymonde's house and got to meet his family. With kids ranging in age from two to sixteen, it was beautiful to see so much love flowing through their home and another reminder of why I had written that note praying for peace in the Middle East.

With two weeks left of our trip, we decided to cancel our plans for Greece and return to London instead. With only a couple of hundred dollars in the kitty, we phoned my dad to ask him to send us some money. After checking into our hotel that was just around the corner from the famous Walkabout Club, we trekked the five kilometres (didn't want to waste our pennies on buses) to the bank to see if our money had arrived.

They couldn't find it. Nothing.

For a week straight, we checked every day, but evidently the money was stuck in a drawer or hanging out in limbo. Skint, Paul asked his mum to send money, but that took forever too. We ended up having to extend our trip by two weeks because we could literally not check out of our hotel due to our inability to pay the bill. All we could do was go for walks and eat Wendy's burgers (which make McDonald's look like a hatted restaurant) and onion bhajis. I've never felt so helpless in my life.

Once again, Paul and I went to the bank to see if any money had arrived and hallelujah – we had $6000 waiting for us! Feeling flush, we paid our hotel bill, hired a car and spent a week and a half driving around England. This time we met my relatives in Cambridge and Birmingham before winding our way back through beautiful Devon and Cornwall. As our first overseas trip as a couple came to a close, I knew there was no one else I'd rather take an Olympic Airlines flight with.

By the time we got back to Melbourne, Paul and I were broke and in debt to our parents. Paul got a day job working at his cousin's company, On Hold Communications (which sounds like an oxymoron), but continued to do music for my shows at night. Seeing as any job that required attire suitable for an office setting was out of the question for me, I went back to the comedy scene and started working with Gibbo, Sal and Scotty (all friends and colleagues from my MRPG days) on a revival of the MRPG's the *Natural Normans*.

The original line-up included a girl named Fran, but she had just had a baby and wasn't interested in dressing in drag and singing sexist songs anymore. (I also don't think spending her days smoking pot and writing ridiculous parodies would have been very socially acceptable now that she was a breastfeeding mother.) The *Natural Normans* proved to be a huge hit. After doing shows at venues like Le Joke, the Albion, the Prince Patrick Hotel, the Espy and the Last Laugh, we started getting MC jobs and were eventually approached by Nanette, who wanted to be our manager/agent.

While the *Natural Normans* was our main act, Sal and I also created numerous sketches with two of my favourite characters: May Day and Gail Force Wind. They were similar to *The Bitches*, but with more structure. They operated under the name *Dags in Full Flight*. Pretty quickly, we got enough publicity that Nanette convinced us we needed to take the *Natural Normans* on the comedy festival circuit.

As an up-and-coming comedy troupe in the late 1980s/early 1990s, getting invited or accepted to a comedy festival was pretty much the equivalent of getting a Netflix special today. Feeling motivated and pumped to give it our all, we managed to book Edinburgh, Melbourne, Perth and Adelaide. Since most of these festivals only paid for big names, we knew we'd have to do quite a few side gigs to fund these trips.

First up: a comedy showcase at RMIT (Royal Melbourne Institute of Technology) alongside the Doug Anthony All Stars and the country's most beloved baldy, Flacco, who was created by Paul Livingston. In terms of seniority, the Doug Anthony All Stars were the clear headliner, with the *Natural Normans* and Flacco as openers. I don't know who raised the students at RMIT, but their behaviour was abhorrent. Within minutes of Flacco taking the stage with his signature bald head marked with a single curly Q of hair, the audience began booing and then eventually shouting (warning: bad word alert), 'Get off the stage, you baldy c***!'

Terrified for how four women in drag would be received by this less than gracious crowd, we timidly ran onstage for our set. Straight away, we could tell they didn't like us. After singing a few songs, the boos echoed off the walls and caused us to grow silent. That's when the chanting started.

'Bring back the baldy c***! Bring back the baldy c***!'

'So no encore?' I asked before running off the stage through a hail of beer cans.

Clearly the RMIT kids only wanted one thing: the Doug Anthony All Stars.

It sucks not being loved and adored, but at least we got paid and were that much closer to our next stop: the Edinburgh Fringe Festival. In our eyes, this was the Big Kahuna and we worked day and night on a show called *Dog's Breakfast*. Sadly, Scotty (Denise) decided to stay behind because she had two young kids. (You'll be pleased to learn that Denise got to perform in the 2012 Edinburgh Fringe, proving good things really do come to those who wait.)

Even though the *Natural Normans* was down one Norman, we

were still pumped to share the festival program with (our unofficial rivals) the Doug Anthony All Stars, as well as comedians like Denis Leary, Julian Clary and Rachel Berger, and troupes such as the Fabulous Singlettes and Found Objects. Our trip lasted four weeks in total and was everything I could have ever wanted.

Since we were strapped for cash, our partners stayed in Australia and we all booked a giant Edwardian share house. I bunked with Dave Taranto, who was a reporter for RRR and *The Age*, and Colin Lane. I'm pretty sure Sal had a room with Rachel Berger, but Rachel left the house and got a hotel room because it was too cramped, smelled like gas and she was used to living by herself. Even though we were in our thirties, it was like college all over again.

When we weren't living our best lives onstage, we were usually out partying with the other performers in the assembly rooms. One night, Alan Bates (who went on to be *the* Sir Alan Bates) had just done a one-man show and Gibbo, who could only be described as maggotted, waltzed over and said in an empathetic tone, 'You look absolutely exhausted. You need a bath.' Alan had a perplexed look on his face as Gibbo proceeded to help him stand. 'I'm taking you to a taxi right now. It's time to go home, have a bath and relax.'

The next morning, when we were doing the fun recap of the night, Gibbo stated, 'I can't be sure, but I think I might have sent

Alan Bates home in a taxi to have a bath last night.' God, I loved her. She was so brave, so loud and so free. I loved her as Matron Conniving Bitch in *Let The Blood Run Free* and as the neighbour in *The Castle* and so much more. She taught me a lot about being courageous, big and silly. Gone far too soon, the world is a less funny place without the lovely Gibbo.

These women were the type of people you'd want by your side during a night on the booze. One night at Falls Creek I drank a whole bottle of apple schnapps and could not stop vomiting for twelve hours. We were supposed to perform a *Natural Normans* show that night, but I was so out of it, Scotty had to drag me through the snow to a doctor's surgery. To everyone in the waiting room's horror, I dry retched until I was finally seen and given an injection, which seemed to work. I went home, slept for three hours and then murdered a toasted sandwich. This is the only time I truly didn't care if the show went on or not.

But magically it did.

While the douchebags at RMIT didn't think we were funny, the people of Edinburgh did. *Dog's Breakfast* (which featured Rachel Berger, the Found Objects troupe and three-quarters of the *Natural Normans*) made it into the top six of the Perrier Comedy Awards. (Think gold Logie! Think Oscar! Think Pulitzer Prize!) Ultimately the win went to a French circus called Cirque Archaos. They're known as the pioneers of the contemporary circuses we know today, so we weren't too bummed to lose to a bunch of people who juggled chainsaws, rode dirt bikes on high wires and contorted themselves in Kama Sutric ways that make you think they're made of rubber ... After all, we were just a bunch of ragtag Aussies who liked to act the fool and make people laugh.

Back in Melbourne, we were all starting to feel the effects of our time in Edinburgh. Our agent, Nanette, was calling left, right and centre with auditions for plays, films and TV shows. The first role I won was for two episodes as a mother of a young asthmatic girl in *The Flying Doctors*. Even though I'd been acting for years by this stage, truthfully, I didn't know what the hell was going on during the first day on set. Between being told to lower my voice and stop leaping around and overacting (I thought I was being pretty minimalist to be honest) and being reminded to not 'barrel' the camera, I quickly learnt that TV is a whole other kettle of fish.

Fortunately, the wonderful Bill Hughes was directing my episodes and gave me so much helpful advice and encouragement. He's since directed me on *Home and Away*. The funny thing about performing in your thirties is that there's an unspoken assumption that because of your age you should know what you're doing. For me, nothing could have been further from the truth. I'm eternally grateful for the likes of Bill, Colin, Kevin,

Doreen, Gibbo, Sal, Scotty ... the list goes on ... for all the tools and the confidence I needed to keep showing up to film sets and muddling my way through.

While I loved my brief TV experience, I still felt most at home while onstage doing comedy. To be honest, we were so willing to act like fools because we simply loved it. The definition of total budget comedy, we weren't in it expecting to make a fortune. We just wanted to make people laugh in exchange for copious amounts of attention and praise. Is that too much to ask?

Turns out that was a perfectly acceptable request at both the Melbourne and Perth comedy festivals. Adelaide? Not so much. While the crowd was receptive and seemed okay at the time, the write-ups we received made us think they simply didn't get the gag. (Women dressed as men taking the piss out of sexist songs. What's not to get?) Upon further investigation, we discovered that the paper had sent the amateur weekly food critic to do our review.

'It was like watching four Benny Hills onstage.'

It was intended as a blatant insult, but as lovers of British slapstick comedy, we were flattered!

CHAPTER 9
How to Stay Safe Doing Stand-Up

While I was getting my ego bruised in Adelaide, Paul took time to visit his nephews and niece in Albury–Wodonga. When we both got home to Melbourne, Paul went on and on about his family and how nice it was to be around kids. Then, just as casually as you'd suggest a weekend trip to IKEA, he asked, 'Maybe we could have a baby?'

Perhaps it was my brief time as a teacher, but having children wasn't on my to-do list. On top of my general aversion to sticky hands, endless questions and vomit and poo (especially other people's), having a baby would mean less time for my favourite subjects: friends, weed, musical theatre, comedy and me. I often think of the quote from *Overboard* when Goldie Hawn's mother (played by the iconic Katherine Helmond) says, 'But darling, if you have a baby, *you* won't be the baby anymore!'

Part of me was worried about how drastically my lifestyle would be affected. Theatre and comedy happen at odd hours, require loads of travel and aren't that conducive to motherhood. Full of doubts, I was surprised when my response to Paul's question was, 'You know what? I'm thirty-seven. I think we better get cracking.'

Two weeks later I was on location in Daylesford in Victoria shooting scenes for a short film. It was May and absolutely freezing. While in my cabin getting changed, something in my peripheral vision caught my eye. I had to do a double take. What looked like two Oreos floating in space was actually the reflection in the mirror of my nipples! This might be too much information, but I usually have small, pale-pink nipples. You seriously have to look twice to see them. All of a sudden they were loud and proud and bearing resemblance to those of a gorilla. Convinced that such a change in my areolae was a sure sign I was pregnant, I got a test the next day.

Two pink lines.

In disbelief, once back in Melbourne, I went to the doctor

and they confirmed what the home test had already confirmed: I was still pregnant. Equal parts elated, terrified and shocked, I sat Paul down to tell him the news.

'What? Oh my God! So fast!'

'I know,' I said, still baffled that we had instantly made a baby.

'Does this mean we should get married?'

'I don't know. Do we need more white goods?'

'Nah,' Paul said and smiled.

We were overjoyed and overwhelmed and began doing all the stuff soon-to-be parents do. We bought baby books, signed up for birthing classes and started brainstorming baby names. For no reason whatsoever, I was convinced we were having a boy. However, I really wanted a girl. One night while Paul and I were watching the finale of one of those search for a star shows, the winner was a girl named Clancy. My all-time favourite Australian poem is 'Clancy of the Overflow' by Banjo Paterson, but it had never occurred to me a girl could be called Clancy until this moment.

As the show ended and everyone cheered for Clancy, I declared, 'If we have a girl, we're calling her Clancy.'

Paul rolled his eyes. 'Over my dead body.'

Before I could say that that could be arranged, Paul suggested Chloe instead.

While I did like the name Chloe and toyed with it for a few months, my sister and pretty much every friend kept pointing out that Olivia Newton-John had a daughter with the very same name. Because of her popularity, subsequently even the dogs were barking 'Chloe'. As someone with the most common name ever (you've seen how many Lynnes are mentioned in this book), I really wanted something that was different. For the moment, we shelved the debate because after all, we could have been having a boy anyway.

My enthusiasm for the life growing inside me diminished slightly when I began experiencing morning sickness. The non-stop nausea made me dependent on bedside crackers, cold toast and the avoidance of pretty much all cooked food. The excitement of being with child was also dulled every time we went to the doctor who insisted on referring to my 'geriatric pregnancy'. (Aren't your late thirties already hard enough?)

By the second trimester, the nausea had subsided and my appetite had returned. This puts a look of horror on most people's faces now, but since you need lots of iron when you're pregnant, I lived on lashings of homemade pâté. (The other sources I knew about – lamb's fry, kidneys or any other type of offal besides liver – were not something I was willing to put into my mouth.) Obviously, we now know pâté is full of vitamin A and not ideal for pregnant women when eaten in large quantities.

Come to think of it, I remember also eating a lot of bean sprouts. Whoops. The pâté must have been overkill because when I had my bloodwork done during my second trimester the nurse did it twice because my iron levels were so high. She told me I had enough iron for all the women in the hospital. Funny how pregnancy diet rules change. And only funny because – spoiler alert – I gave birth to a healthy baby.

As my belly began to grow, so did my desire to return to the stage. While theatre was still a huge passion, I couldn't wait to get back to the comedy circuit. During my time in Melbourne and at the MRPG, I'd grown to love live, dangerous and stupid comedy, which is why it made sense when I announced to Paul that I wanted to try my hand at stand-up. Stand-up had always been terrifying unchartered territory, but for some reason I felt less vulnerable doing it as a pregnant woman. It's like I had a belly of armour to literally stand behind.

With my guitar in hand, I sat down to write a 'Tight Twenty'. Just like it sounds, it's a twenty-minute comedy routine. Since writing parodies was a skill I had learnt while moonlighting at teachers' college and honed at the MRPG, it felt natural to include musical elements in my set. Finally confident with my act, I got a spot for first timers at the Albion Hotel in Fitzroy where the seasoned comedian, Richard Stubbs, was also performing. He was the master of relatable everyday comedy.

Unlike every other time I had prepared to walk out onstage, I was nervous. Like jumping out of a plane nervous. The only thing that put me at ease was the thought that surely no one would be mean or throw something at a pregnant woman. Over the next twenty minutes I made jokes about my pregnancy, sang silly songs and ultimately received a very warm response. Proud and relieved that nobody booed me, I left feeling exhilarated, invincible and excited to do it all again.

While many of my future shows were much the same, I quickly discovered that people *will* throw empty beer cans and rolled-up programs at a pregnant woman if they don't think you're funny. It was nonsensical how in some venues I was the funniest human on the planet and in others I might as well have been onstage silently doing my taxes. Some days I'd walk around feeling like the next Carol Burnett and other days I just wanted to open a vein because it was such an ego-crushing endeavour.

Determined to power on, I was thrilled when I was asked to MC a comedy show at the Hilton with Rich Hall as the headliner. At this point, I was nearly six months pregnant and looking every bit of it in my circa 1960s vintage black velvet dress that I had recently found in an op shop. My job was relatively easy: simply walk on, crack a few jokes, introduce Rich and then leave.

Simple, right?

Well, as I attempted to walk down the carpeted stairs, my

heel got stuck in a carpet loop and I took flight. Yet again, those skinny things dangling from my bum failed to support me. (Could also have been the fact that I'd chosen five-inch high heels …) Anyway, as you can imagine the show shuddered to a halt as the crowd watched my face, baby bump and knees smack every step on the staircase. I was literally laid out on my protruding stomach like a human Bosu ball.

Numerous people ran to help me up and helped me backstage where my bloody and carpet-burned legs were bandaged up and I was given a cup of tea. Normally one might be embarrassed by such a public fall, but all I could think about was my baby. If I didn't lose him or her after that, they must be hanging in there big time. I went to the bathroom to make sure there wasn't any spotting and then went home. I've always been one to trust my instincts and I truly felt like everything was okay. However, it was a big reminder to stop falling down stairs.

The next day I went to the doctor for a check-up. Thank God, he confirmed that my baby's heart was still beating. Feeling an enormous amount of relief from having survived such an ordeal, I took a moment to reflect on my life choices. I came to the decision that I was now done with stand-up. I'd conquered a fear, ticked off another item on my bucket list and was at a point in my pregnancy (and life), where I didn't need any more adrenaline.

People often ask me if I'd ever do stand-up again and the

answer is never. (Well, probably not.) Stand-up gave me some of my highest highs and lowest lows. I like to remember the good times, forget the bad and not tempt fate in that way. It's one of the things that made me appreciate bravery. I've also learnt that I'm not the type of person who needs to face every fear. For example, I loathe heights so I will never go sky-diving. And I hate spiders, so don't expect me to go all Bear Grylls and eat one if I'm ever lost in the wilderness.

During my third trimester I was blessed with heartburn and leg cramps. I spent those twelve weeks sleeping in a V shape. To achieve this, I had to use no fewer than eight pillows shoved strategically under my back and head to elevate my chest to alleviate the heartburn while pillows placed under my legs and feet were to help with my cramps. The annoying thing was that just as I'd get comfortable, I'd have to get up and wee.

On one of the rare occasions I did venture out to do something social – on this occasion to watch Shirley MacLaine perform – I received a series of dirty looks from fellow audience members – all because I was sipping Gaviscon from a brown paper bag! I thought I was being discreet about my pregnancy ailments, while they thought I was hitting the grog. With hindsight, I'm not sure why I was hiding my antacid in a brown paper bag.

By the time my due date came and passed, I had gone over my perfect birth scenario roughly 936 times. In my mind, my waters would break while I was sleeping. Paul and I would then grab my pre-packed bag and head to the hospital where I'd give birth vaginally and without drugs. I imagined that through my Lamaze breathing, Paul's support and my pre-emptive perineal massage (which I highly recommend … if you can reach it), I would positively jog around the birthing suite and then squat my baby out.

Like most expectations versus reality scenarios, my labour and delivery unfolded somewhat differently.

Instead of being blissfully asleep when I went into labour, I was eight days overdue and standing stark naked next to a water cooler in our living room on a 42-degree day. This scene lasted from Friday morning to Sunday evening and only varied when I was naked and playing scrabble, naked and screaming, naked and in the bath (which they tell you not to do because you might miss your water breaking), naked and having awkward sex to try to speed things up (nearly impossible when you have a land mass attached to your torso), or wandering around the neighbourhood. (Clothed, thank you very much.) With my contractions all over the shop, and my discomfort reaching uncharted levels, Paul called the hospital to give our midwife an update. I could hear her voice through the phone.

'First labours are long. Just be patient and tell her to take some Panadol.'

The opposite of satisfied with her answer, I went to scream that 'Panadol's not going to cut it – I'm up to pussy's bow and it's effing time!', when all of a sudden: *whoosh*. My waters broke. Paul relayed the news and we finally got the go ahead to come on down.

As water cascaded down my legs, Paul got me clothed in pyjamas and (as instructed) diapered me in a maternity pad so the midwife could check the quality of my waters. Contracting at home is one thing, contracting in a car with your bum in the back window is quite another. I don't know what the other drivers saw, but the view would have been quite alarming I'm sure.

Once admitted and examined, it was discovered that there was meconium in my waters. This meant my dreams of jogging around the delivery suite were dashed. I was laid flat on my back, hooked up to every machine that went 'ping', given pethidine (thank you), as well as gas to suck on.

Six hours of squeezing the life out of Paul's arms and neck later, I was able to push and push and push and at 6.37 a.m. on 28 January 1991 we met our darling baby girl. Our moment of euphoria was short-lived because my blood pressure shot up to 200 over 100. Paul kept watch over the baby in the hospital nursery while I was taken to the ICU and remained extremely out of it for the next seven hours.

When I was finally able to look in a mirror, I barely recognised the woman staring back at me. I had burst so many blood vessels in my face while pushing that I was left looking like a middle-aged Pippi Longstocking. Too tired to care and anxious to get to my baby, I was finally wheeled to our room, which we shared with two other new mothers.

For the next twenty-four hours I held, nursed and stared at my daughter. I took in every inch of her, including her sweet hands that were clasped in a way that reminded me of Mother Teresa. It was crazy to think that I never wanted to be a mum, because once I held her, I knew there was no other way for my life to be.

The next day, I turned thirty-eight and couldn't have asked for a better gift than a baby girl … who remained nameless for nine days. Everyone kept saying, 'You'll know what name to choose once you see them.' That's bullshit. (I mean, come on, what baby comes out looking like an Edith, Gertrude, or Cletus?) After we counted ten little fingers, ten little toes, and ten of Paul's bruises, we went home where we spent the next week trying to figure out how to care for our little human, whom we referred to as 'little lamb', 'little pumpkin' and 'little peanut'. In other words, pretty much any little animal, food or inanimate object we could think of.

On day nine we decided it was time to give her an actual name, so like most sophisticated baby-naming activities, we laid her in the middle of the bed and put a folded piece of paper with the name 'Clancy' on one side and a folded piece of paper with the name 'Chloe' on the other. Whichever way she slightly turned/rolled we would go with that. After debating which awkward newborn jolt counted, it was determined she turned left.

Paul picked up the piece of paper. 'Clancy!'

I was thrilled.

Only years later did he tell me it was actually Chloe.

☆ ☆ ☆

Like most new mums, I adjusted to motherhood. I sobbed my way through the third day blues, obsessively checked that Clancy was still breathing, and constantly wondered how on earth I was going to keep this thing alive and help her become a confident, strong and independent woman (without giving her too much material for her therapist). No pressure. Paul was just as clueless. If only kids came with a manual.

But thank God *everyone* else has an opinion on how to raise them.

Mum came down from Sydney to ease our sense of panic.

While she wasn't one to sit you down for a deep and meaningful conversation at the kitchen bench, she was very intuitive when it came to knowing how to lighten my load, leave the room when needed and of course bring me snacks. Eventually she had to go home and Paul needed to get back to work, which meant it was officially time for me to find my groove.

Never one to sit still, I decided that I'd get Clancy in the pram for a trip to Box Hill. Over the next few months this became a bit of a weekly ritual for us. I loved looking in shops and eating sultana donuts, but most of all, I loved showing Clancy off. People would generally *ooh* and *ahh* over my darling girl, but sometimes I'd get the following from little old ladies.

'Aw, is that your grandson?'

(To be fair, I was thirty-eight and all the other mums were like fifteen.)

'No, she's actually mine. And it's a girl.'

'What's her name?'

'Clancy.'

'Aw, Clarence! What a strong name for such a fine young boy.'

Eventually I'd just give up, take a bite of my donut and continue strolling my grandson around the shopping centre.

Thanks to one of Paul's great aunts, who generously left him an inheritance, home ownership came on the cards for us in late 1991. We decided to buy a recently renovated, single-storey, two-bedroom home in the northern suburb of Thornbury, mainly because it had a granny flat that we could rent out. (Aside from not doing a background check and renting it out to criminals who robbed the neighbourhood blind of garden tools, our decision to buy a place with an income opportunity proved to be financially beneficial!) I loved this house because it had a great big open-plan kitchen–living area as well as a back verandah stretching the length of the house.

The best part though was my neighbour, Libby. I had a now six-month-old Clancy and she had a six-month-old Naomi. While most people hate being able to see directly into their neighbour's yard, I loved it. For starters, Libby could see when I was struggling so she'd yell for me to drop Clancy over the fence to play with Naomi. This woman was literally my saviour. She was very 'Mother Earth' and made sure I was well fed and had time to run errands while Paul worked. Even after Libby went on to have two more kids, she managed to make motherhood look like a breeze. It's weird how being with a baby all day long can feel isolating. Perhaps it was my lack of interaction with babies that made the experience feel alien.

On top of relying on Libby, I also joined a mother's group,

where I discovered far too late that Clancy needed to be doing tummy time. Who knew? I always laid her on her back in the bassinet or pram. It never occurred to me to put her on her tummy on the floor. When I finally did try, she screamed the house down. Luckily, her lack of tummy time wasn't too detrimental, and the funny thing is that these days Clancy is making up for lost time by spending her career on the floor teaching Pilates and yoga.

If there was one thing I learnt from that first year, it's that there's no harm in getting peace of mind. I don't want to gloat, but Clancy slept through the night pretty much from six weeks on. However one evening she stayed asleep from 10 p.m. until 11 a.m. Concerned (but not enough to attempt waking her), I called the Emergency Mothers' Panic Line (which I'm sure is not actually called that) to explain that my baby had been sleeping for a *very* long time.

'Is she breathing?' the midwife asked.

'Yes.'

'Is she blue?'

'No.'

'Then stop your bloody complaining, you stupid woman!'

For the most part, I think I was a relaxed mother. Not overly patient, but my anxious moments were few and far between, even though the world seemed to be trying to scare the crap out of me. From people telling you horror stories about miscarriages and SIDS to tales of cats sitting on a baby's face, it's rather hard to enjoy the ride when everyone keeps telling you you're going to fall off.

'Irrational fears' seems to be the name of the game and if needing to show your baby's poop-filled nappy to a group of women at a park to get confirmation that the consistency and colour look normal is what makes you feel at peace, then you have to do what you have to do.

Sometimes it's also leaving your screaming baby with your partner so you can go chain-smoke in the backyard.

The good news is you eventually learn how to tune out the chatter and you regain some sense of normalcy. Soon after we moved into our house in Thornbury, I started doing plays again and going for auditions in film and television. Finally feeling like some version of my old self, I relished every second I got to perform. With Paul still working in communications during the day, it was so nice knowing I could count on him to watch Clancy in the evenings when I'd go to rehearsal.

One night while chatting about how much he hated his job and how I wasn't really cut out to be a stay-at-home mum for the next eighteen years, a thought popped into my head.

'You know what? I need to get a job on a soap opera. Then you could stay at home with Clancy and be a house husband.'

He didn't hate the idea.

My next audition was not for TV, but for a show in development called *Daily Grind* at the Melbourne Workers Theatre. It was about two strippers, one ageing and a lover of burlesque and one new, young and into working *hot*. As opposed to cheeky burlesque, which is more like teasing nudity, *hot* is all about shaved pink bits right in your face. Thankfully, I was cast to play the ageing stripper (much better at teasing) opposite the wonderful Belinda McClory as the hot youngster. The play was written by ex-stripper Vicki Reynolds, who had recently died of breast cancer. With Lisa Dombroski set to direct the play and Vicki's estate allowing us free rein to workshop it, we worked hard to create a piece that would pay homage to the incredible life Vicki had lived.

At this point, Clancy was about twelve months old, but for some reason I still looked like I was eight months pregnant. When you're the size of a small African nation and anxious there'd be nowhere to hide while wearing stripper clothes under stage lights, you take action. Drastic action.

So I made a serious investment: Aerobics Oz Style videos.

The commercials had been looping on my TV for years and I always just sort of gawked at them, but at this moment I was desperate for whatever June Jones and Wendi Carroll were selling.

Like most things bought from TV, these videos were used once and then sat untouched until Clancy made me put them in a garage sale we had in 2006.

The good news is that three months of learning intense stripper choreography can and will get you back to your pre-baby body! The show was a success and attracted audience members like TV producer Bob Weis. After watching the chemistry between Belinda and me onstage, he wanted to cast us as a mother and daughter in a miniseries he was working on called *Seven Deadly Sins*.

Since I was planning to fly up to Sydney for my brother-in-law's fortieth in the following week, I was able to book a time to audition while there. Unfortunately, while at the birthday party, my love of finger foods got the best of me. I don't know what I ate, probably some dodgy spring roll, but something made me violently ill for three days. I'm talking *The Exorcist* type of projectile vomiting, bowel movements that require showers and intense nausea that makes you want to throw yourself in front of a coal train.

After seventy-two hours of food poisoning, I summoned every ounce of strength I could muster to get up, bathe, put on clothing and drag myself to the audition. Looking like I was on death's doorstep, I entered the room and was greeted by the director Di Drew, and casting director Liz Mullinar. Feeling weak, dizzy and completely unqualified, I somehow made it through my lines.

When the read through was done, and feeling like I'd totally stuffed it up, I did the one thing they tell you never to do in drama school – make an excuse. I told Di and Liz I'd been violently ill for the past three days and that was why my performance might not have been up to par.

Evidently, it didn't matter.

I was cast as the mother in the 'Gluttony' episode!

But then it got even better. Not two weeks later, my agent rang and said that Liz Mullinar wanted me to audition for a role on a soap opera called *Home and Away*.

'It's only a guest spot, but it might have the potential to be ongoing. You'd be replacing Jacquy Phillips, who played Irene for a short stint. Anyway, Liz is down in Melbourne for the week so you can do the audition there. I'll send you the character breakdown ASAP.'

The breakdown was unforgettable. And succinct.

Irene: Thin, wasted alcoholic.

Still looking and feeling like crap from the bout of food poisoning, I suddenly understood why Liz had thought of me for the role. I went down to a studio in South Melbourne expecting a cattle call, but it was just me, a microphone and Liz manning a camera. I did a scene where I'm asking, actually begging, for forgiveness from my three children. (For trying to push them down the stairs while I was drunk, if you were wondering.)

Liz hit stop on her camera. 'That was pretty good, I think they'll like that ...'

I left the studio feeling positive about my performance and a little bewildered by the whole process. For something that was such a big deal, the audition felt astonishingly low-key. That's the thing about Liz, though – no matter who you were, she always made you feel comfortable and like you weren't wasting her time.

Over the next few days, I was conscious of not getting my hopes up, but couldn't help feeling giddy every time the phone rang. Like any sane actress waiting to hear how an audition went, when the phone did finally ring and I happened to be in the shower, I jumped out completely naked and soaking wet and sprinted to answer it.

'You've got the role!' rang in my ears for the rest of the day.

CHAPTER 10
Becoming Irene

While looking like a thin, wasted alcoholic got me onto the *Home and Away* set, my transformation into Irene Roberts (a working-class, cigarette-smoking, loud-mouthed, brassy Aussie battler who had once tried to throttle her kids and was now desperately trying to stay on the wagon) would take a vat of peroxide, an impressive collection of gold hoop earrings and tubs of pale blue eyeshadow ... and pale green too because sometimes she liked to mix it up. It would also take mental rummaging through the vast collection of my parents' often bizarre Australian colloquialisms and turns of phrases, if I was going to grab this character by the throat and dive in boots and all. (Because I've always loved a mixed metaphor.)

Prior to auditioning and getting offered the role, Paul and I had caught an episode of *Home and Away* here and there, but never really watched the show and truthfully had no idea what was going on. Eager to front up on day one able to pass the toughest of *Home and Away* trivia tests, I started religiously watching the show as well as asking avid fans I knew to fill me in on what had happened over the past five or so years.

Worried I'd subconsciously imitate Jacquy Phillips' original portrayal of Irene, I purposely skipped her episodes. From what I gathered, though, Irene was a viciously mean drunk and easy to hate.

From time to time, I've wondered why Jacquy didn't want to reprise the role. Was it the heavy themes? Was she tired of playing such a rough character? Was she sick of being abused in the supermarket because Irene tried to push a teenager down the stairs in a drunken rage? (It's amazing how much people can hate you in real life for something your character did.) Or perhaps she wanted to protect her vocal cords for her return to the stage because let's be honest: there's a lot of yelling on soaps. (And lies, deception, unplanned pregnancies, stabbings, comas, shootings, poisonings, runaways, cancer, affairs, car accidents, hijackings, sexual assaults, incest, kidnappings, people coming back from the dead and ghosts morphing out of white goods.)

There are also a lot of lines ... usually accompanied by ominous music. For a show that only has twenty-two-minute episodes, the writers manage to weave more drama together than a week in state politics.

Even though I was thoroughly entertained, I think I made it through about six episodes before giving up on trying to figure out what in the blue blazes was going on. I also needed to focus on the logistics of moving from Melbourne to Sydney for three months of filming.

Since I was only doing a guest role, Paul and I agreed that it made sense if he stayed in Melbourne and continued working while I took a now twenty-month-old Clancy with me to stay with my parents in a townhouse they'd bought in Sans Souci. Mum was sold on the suburb. Dad was sold on the spa. I was sold on their endless love and willingness to watch Clancy while I went to work.

From my brief experience on *The Flying Doctors* and *Seven Deadly Sins*, I knew that the hours that go into filming a single episode are brutally long. As a mother, the idea of being away from my toddler made me feel anxious and guilty, but I felt like this was an opportunity that may not come around again. It was a guest role. I was sure to be back in Melbourne in no time.

With our bags packed full of sippy cups, toys, clothes as well as my panic and paranoia, Clancy and I flew up to Sydney in October 1992.

On my first ever drive to the former Channel 7 Studios in Epping, I couldn't help but feel a mixture of emotions: excited, petrified, guilty, entitled, fraudulent, talented, lucky, grateful, regretful and of course – hungry. Too anxious to eat, I tried to take deep breaths and remind myself that they must have hired me for a reason.

Adopting a fake it till you make it attitude, I remember checking my make-up in the car's rear-view mirror and then proudly walking into the studio where I was greeted by a flurry of fast-talking people who seemed to know what was going on. I did my best to keep up with a nice lady called Sherree, who was having me pop in and out of green rooms and dressing rooms to meet other actors like Judy Nunn, Ray Meagher and of course my onscreen kids. As I did my best to remember names and act like I wasn't completely intimidated, someone else came by carrying a stack of papers that stretched from his belt to his chin.

'Lynne! Hi, nice to meet you! Here are your scripts for this week's episodes.'

I'm not kidding when I say there were a couple of trees' worth of scripts in his arms. (Okay, small trees.) Again, trying to act like I wasn't at all horrified by the sheer amount of pages, I smiled and reached for them. In a quick exchange, I learnt that *Home and Away* films five episodes every week, but that I was only slated to be in three per week. While trying to compute how many trees have to die for actors in all five episodes, a bubbly make-up artist summoned me into her den. There I met even more people who knew what they were doing. To me.

'Blonde hair, black roots.'

'Blue eyeshadow. The kind that makes you look *battered.*'

'She needs to look how vodka smells.'

'Do you have anything to highlight her failures in life?'

Okay, so these exact words didn't really come out of their mouths, but I swear that's what they were thinking because over the next three hours my hair, skin, nails and wardrobe went through a make-under of epic proportions. With my hair deep-fried and coiffed to exude recovering alcoholic meets do-it-yourself-at-home-bleach-job meets forgiveness-seeking mother, I tried on outfits that can only be described as white trailer trash. Think vibrant stripes, high-waisted jeans and bucket hats teamed with 1970s throwbacks like denim miniskirts. My favourite was the abundance of faux leather jerkins that made Irene look like she could pick up part-time work at a medieval jousting tournament.

With the producers satisfied with my transformation, the next stop was rehearsals, which were held at the imposing Eastwood

Masonic temple. With the set taped out on the floor, the cast would run through each scene, discuss our characters and hastily write down 'blocking' (which refers to how an actor moves through a scene) on our scripts as if our lives depended on it. While blocking is important in theatre, it's not a huge deal if you step too far or decide to improvise a hand gesture. In TV, however, if a show uses Steadicam, blocking is crucial because just like it sounds – a Steadicam stays still and you need to stay in the frame.

Nearly every time I was on set the director would have to yell at me, 'Find your mark!' I wanted the studio floor to open up and swallow me. I'm pretty sure I visibly shook for the first few months I worked on the show. I was like Katharine Hepburn without the acting talent. And it didn't help that one or two of the established cast members made it seem like I should have known better.

Even though my first day on set went okay, I couldn't shake the sense of imposter syndrome. I drove home feeling relieved and excited yet strangely terrified of what lay ahead. When I entered my parents' house I saw Clancy happily eating dinner, which momentarily gave me pause. Had my mother cooked something edible? Then I saw the box of frozen fish sticks and all was right in the world again.

As I walked over to give Clancy a cuddle, she gave me a

perplexed look that clearly said, 'Um, why did you go to work as a brunette and come home looking like a $20 hooker?' For the next ten minutes she hid her face in her highchair and refused to look at me. Maternal guilt made me wonder if it was my hair or the fact that I had been gone for the past twelve hours.

'I forgot to tell you ...' Mum shouted from the kitchen.

'What?' I asked while trying to earn Clancy's trust back.

'Clancy's potty-trained! I took her nappy off this morning and she used the toilet all day. No accidents.'

'That's amazing!' I said trying to fake an excited tone.

I know I should have been beyond grateful that my mum had potty-trained my daughter in a day, but I weirdly felt like I'd missed a milestone I was supposed to reach. Boom. More guilt.

One of the things I find annoying about 'mother guilt' is that men rarely share the emotional burden. Gender stereotypes usually dictate that when a dad leaves for a business trip it's no big deal because that's what dads do. But when a mum leaves it's like, 'who's looking after the children?' Uh, the other parent? There are two parents for a reason, right? (Or family members, nannies and boarding schools ...)

Anyway, I'm starting this rant because by the time my episode hit the airwaves, Channel 7's PR team had been spruiking me big time. It seemed like every gossip mag I picked up had photos of my face on them or in them. *Irene Roberts: Back in Summer Bay.*

For the most part, when you're a stage actor, you have anonymity. But when you're on national television, let alone a successful series, then you just can't avoid the whole recognition thing.

The press continued to ramp up when I was offered a contract to reprise my role as Irene for another twelve months. This meant that in August 1993, Paul quit his job and moved to Sydney so I could work on *Home and Away* and he could look after Clancy full-time. (God *was* listening!) Little did I know, due to my naivety in interviews, this would be the story that the press chose to focus on.

Reporter: 'Ms McGranger, now that you're starring as Irene in *Home and Away*, how are you coping with being a mum both on and off screen?'

Naive Lynne: 'It's actually really hard and I'm riddled with guilt. Luckily, my partner Paul, whom I'm not married to, is happy to stay home and be a house husband. I couldn't do it without him!'

At the time I was just being my honest self. Little did I know, this is exactly what the press wanted; vulnerability to turn into next week's headlines:

'Lynne McGranger's starring role in Home and Away *has brought an upheaval in her household. Lynne has just signed on long-term (reportedly five years) to play supposedly reformed*

alcoholic, Irene Roberts. And that means she is now going out to work while her partner Paul stays home and looks after their three-year-old daughter, Clancy.'

'Soap stardom led to role reversal in Lynne McGranger's household!'

'Husband looks after home and young daughter.'

You would have thought I would have learnt from that one, but nope. The next round of interviews went a little something like this:

Reporter: 'Lynne, what's your biggest fear for Clancy?'
Naive Lynne: 'Honestly – a bad body image. With so many women on TV and in magazines looking like heads on sticks, I hope she doesn't compare herself to these unrealistic people ... I struggled with bulimia myself.'

Nek minit ...

'EXTRA EXTRA READ ALL ABOUT IT: Irene's Bulimic Nightmare!'

This puppy garnered a whole two-page spread. While I think it's important to raise awareness about eating disorders, I don't think a journalist dramatising my life in a gossip magazine is the right way to go about it. Going from a relatively quiet life in Melbourne to suddenly having every aspect of my life (laxatives and all) written about without any real commentary from me left me feeling raw and exposed.

As for my relationship, I thought it was a bit ridiculous that they turned my matter-of-fact answers into headlines. But then, I guess our living situation (unmarried, stay-at-home dad, working mum) was a little out of the ordinary to the average Joe. I wish I could say our arrangement was because I was a die-hard feminist intent on smashing the patriarchy. But to be completely honest Paul marches to the beat of his own drum and I'm no domestic goddess. Our lifestyle works because we are both candid and authentic with ourselves and each other about what we want and don't want.

In 1993 I wanted to live and breathe Irene Roberts Monday to Friday and then cuddle my sweet family the rest of the time. Paul was a computer nerd, a willing-with-a-gun-to-his-head grocery shopper and an okay cleaner. (He seemed oblivious to the triffids

The Sensational Spangles in Albury–Wodonga, with a very cute
Django Spangle (aka Paul) in the background, circa 1985.

Paul and me in the sweet bloom of youth (?) and early love. The stylist insisted we both wore lemon. Circa 1985.

Heavily pregnant on a visit to the in-laws. Man, they don't make plastic chairs like that anymore!

Proud mama with a cute Clancy at about five months old at our place in Kew, Melbourne.

A very early *Home and Away* cast shot, circa 1995. Spot the really famous people.

Here we are in *Dick Whittington* at the Brighton Dome in December 1995. Me as Fairy Drag Queen (aka Fairy Bowbells) and Clancy cute as a button in her very first panto. (Mine too, actually!)

Here with the lovely Bec Hewitt (then Cartwright). Not sure of the year or the occasion (probably the late 90s, possibly the Logies).

On *Dancing with the Stars* with Carmelo Pizzino. My fabulous costume and talent for face pulling thankfully distracted people from my terrible cha-cha.

This photo makes me smile. With my beautiful friend Nicky, who fought so bravely, and her beloved first-born, Jack.

My happy place. The last time we visited Maudy and Phil (right and centre back) in York, January 2020. Our friend Jamie (left) was freeloading off them too!

At the footy with our great friend and king of inappropriate Johnny Ruffo.

Left: Even though Carol had resigned as *Home and Away* studio cook during the first lockdown, she still surprised me on set with a birthday cake. What a beautiful lady!
Right: With my gorgeous friend Ada.

Luke, Clancy, me and Paul at the SCG cheering on our Swannies, pre-lockdown.

Love this recent shot of the family (minus my nephew James and Clancy's boyfriend Luke).

growing out of the toilet – however, I was not.) He wanted to look after Clancy and pursue his own projects. I can happily and gratefully say that without Paul I wouldn't be able to sit here and write a memoir about my life as a soap actress for nearly thirty years.

While *Home and Away* has become more work-friendly to mothers it was very hard to try to have it all. I've seen so many young mums come and go due to the inflexibility of the schedule, the gruelling hours that constantly change and the pressure to stay thin. Trying to maintain a Summer Bay body while learning your lines and tending to a sick child who needs to be picked up from day care is not for the fainthearted. (Obviously Irene didn't have the same need-to-look-good-in-a-bikini pressures as many of the younger actresses.) Without help it's impossible. You need someone who can be available for your child inside and outside of day care hours.

For me, that was Paul.

While I was busy trying to redeem the love of my onscreen kids, Nathan, Finlay and Damian, Paul was occasionally cooking, sometimes cleaning and always carting Clancy between pre-school, playdates and after-school activities. He made our house a home, our relationship feel unbeatable and my passion for work utterly validated.

Most of the time I loved this arrangement, but every now

and then I'd wonder if I was missing the little things. Yes, I saw Clancy's first steps, but did I catch every adorable joke she cracked or new trick she learnt? Probably not. What about when she was sad or hurt? Did she secretly wish I was there to comfort her?

On the flipside, when I was with Clancy, I sometimes didn't feel like I was good enough. Once while renting a house in Castle Hill, three-year-old Clancy was running around rudie nudie because it was February and a gazillion degrees outside. As I pottered, I saw her climb up and straddle the velour lounge that Paul's parents had recently handed down to us. Before I could tell her that it wasn't a good idea, she slid down the curved edge and let out a blood-curdling scream.

That's when I saw blood.

Clancy was hysterical.

I was hysterical.

We raced her to Westmead and when we walked through the doors, I could tell it wasn't clear who the patient was. The shock to my system had rendered my skin cadaver-like.

At last, the doctors examined Clancy, while I tried to get my circulation working again. Obviously vaginal injuries to children are suspicious so the doctor started questioning me. Once I explained that she must have caught her little-girl bits on the Velcro of the top of the lounge, the doctor agreed that it was an innocent accident and something that could happen to anyone … Anyone who was naked and straddling a velour lounge. The doctor assured me Clancy would be fine and just to sit her in a warm bath with salt. As for me, they recommended a blood transfusion and a stiff whiskey.

When you compare the above parenting fails and missed milestones to those of Irene, it makes me look like the Mother of the Year. Even though Irene has had some pretty questionable and shudder-worthy moments, I really like her. I like that she's fallible. I like that she calls a spade a front-end loader. You're never going to die wondering what she thinks. Even though she does wrong, she usually means right.

It's been incredible to play and grow alongside a character who is simply living a life. I've said this before, but I always considered myself a performer, not an actor. By the time I had a few years of *Home and Away* under my belt, I really started to grasp the concept that acting is more about listening and reacting and less about face-pulling.

I remember George Burns saying (not to me directly), 'Acting is about the truth and if you can fake that, you've got it made.' Even though I could fake it enough to keep my job, for a long time it didn't feel like I was faking it very well. This sort of self-doubt subsided over the years, but I remember talking to Tony Phelan (who, side note, wanted to leave *Home and Away* so they had a car fall on him aka The Ford of Damocles) in the early 2000s about this very subject.

'Do you ever think, *Oh my God, one day someday someone is going to wake up and realise that I'm faking this and just winging what I do?*' I asked.

Tony laughed and then said in all seriousness, 'There isn't a day that goes by that I haven't had the same thought.'

This meant so much to me because he is held in great esteem as a stage, TV and classical performer. He's done things like *Oedipus*, *King Lear* and other Shakespearian works and has always left audiences in awe. It probably sounds like I'm pissing in his pocket, but he's one of the finest actors I've seen onstage and his frank confession left me feeling less of a charlatan.

I often wonder if people in other professions have the same self-doubt. I think it just comes with the territory of being in a creative industry because your work is going to be subjective and any rejection is going to feel personal. It tends to feel extra personal when some of the people judging you are your peers.

Early on in my tenure as Irene, I developed a condition I like to call the Red Mist. (No, I'm not talking about my menstrual cycle, although the Red Mist is exacerbated if simultaneously experiencing premenstrual syndrome.) Let me describe it for you: the Red Mist is a wave of unrelenting anger that washes over my entire body, flushes blood to my face and starts spinning a web of fiery thoughts in my head.

It's my only kryptonite.

Because Mum raised me well, I'll refrain from naming names; however there have been times on the *Home and Away* set when I felt like a bit of a metaphorical punching bag. Whether it was because they thought my performance was unacceptable or I was perceived as too much of a Pollyanna, I don't know. For what seemed like an eternity, I'd act as a human dartboard for this person's disdain. Eventually, my body developed a physical reaction to this and thus the Red Mist was born. I clearly remember the day when that mist became a full-on cyclone and I finally confronted the individual. Of course, I chose to do it in front of an audience of cast, crew and extras.

'Are you an arsehole to everyone or is it just me?' I asked, trying to appear calm even though my blood had reached Kelvin boiling point.

The individual looked me in the eyes and said, 'No, it's just you.'

Even though those words felt a bit like a twist of an already inserted knife, I breathed a sigh of relief. I had conquered the situation and that person never messed with me again. I don't know if I earnt their respect or if they suddenly realised that being a mean human is no way to go through life, but the next twenty years on *Home and Away* would prove to be a much happier place thanks to the Red Mist.

While the personality clashes and bullshit press headlines were drawbacks of the job, all in all I was having a terrific ride. I loved that Irene would mend relationships, overcome her vices, get into pickles and eventually earn a spot in Australia's heart. I also enjoyed getting to know the wonderful cast members who came and went, and sometimes came again, like Tempany Deckert, Melissa George, Chris Hemsworth, Belinda Emmett, Emily Symons, Kristy Wright, Jessica Tovey ... and so many more (there isn't enough paper in the world to list them all) and, of course, my great friend Ada Nicodemou.

I also enjoyed many of the extracurricular publicity gigs. I remember one time Kate Ritchie, Gary Sweet (who wasn't on the show) and I were invited to be the commentators at Adelaide's annual Christmas Parade. While the organisers and viewers took it very seriously, we didn't. I don't know if it was the giant blow-up Santa marching haphazardly down the street. It might have been the many ways the local dance studios embraced the Christmas spirit by performing as human baubles, human stars, human wreaths, human garlands, and human Christmas presents

(I crossed the line when I said out loud, 'I wonder what those girls have in their boxes!'). Whatever it was, we just couldn't help ourselves and were wetting our pants, blithely taking the mickey.

The parade obviously meant the world to the good people of Adelaide, but clearly we out-of-towners could never do it justice. Since this was airing live on Channel 7, as soon as it was over, we were reprimanded and banned from *ever* being interstate commentators again. This was fine with me because I much preferred promo gigs like being on *Wheel of Fortune* (especially when the other special guests were Eric Bana and Agro), the Channel 7 Perth Telethon or even the Mandurah Crab Festival. (Thank God I didn't have to commentate on that. I was just doing a guest appearance.) Even the old Westfield shopping centre signings were better. However, in 2004, I did agree to be a commentator one last time – at the annual Sydney Gay and Lesbian Mardi Gras (although thankfully I didn't have to say much because the drag queens had it covered).

While it's strange to think that many of my young cast mates grew up doing signings in a Westfield instead of shopping at one with friends, they also had to navigate the press and, like the adults, sometimes received weird stuff from fans. This was pre-9/11 when anthrax wasn't taking over the news so as actors we used to receive and open a lot of our own fan mail. I'll never forget Tammin Sursok receiving an actual bird that was mailed from England. (It was no doubt mailed in good health but sadly lost its will to live somewhere over Darwin before reaching Sydney.)

Speaking of birds, I once mentioned to an English newspaper that we had pet budgies, Princess and Bootie (short for Boutros Boutros Budgie). Shortly after the interview, they were tragically murdered by a neighbourhood dog. Obviously, Paul and I told Clancy that they escaped to get married and live happily ever after in Byron Bay. As if trying to hide the untimely death of a child's pet isn't hard enough, some English fan read the story and started mailing us birdseed. I momentarily thought about calling the newspaper to give them an update, but again, we were trying to keep our cover just in case Clancy ever found out. Actually, I think I need to take a moment to say the following:

Clancy, if you've made it this far into the book, I'm sorry that we lied to you about Princess and Bootie's demise and that you had to find out the truth by reading your mother's memoir.

CHAPTER 11
Me, Myself and Irene

The only time I ever want to give a fan the finger is when they tell me that I sound *exactly* like I do on TV. I know this shouldn't surprise me, but the fact that I sound as ocker in real life as I do in Summer Bay makes me cringe. The only time I want to hug a complete stranger – even in the time of COVID – is when they tell me that I look much younger and thinner in real life. Or that I sound absolutely nothing like Irene. (That hardly ever happens.)

But it's undeniable. After playing the same character for almost three decades, the line between Lynne and Irene has become blurred. I find it gratifying when fans consider us real people who live in a real place. For years, our production coordinator, Sherree Black, would get calls from people asking to book a spot at the Summer Bay Caravan Park. After trying to explain to no avail that it wasn't an *actual* caravan park, just a set, she resorted to telling people, 'Sorry, it's all booked out for this year.'

While most of these interactions are funny and light-hearted, it was rather confronting to start being recognised in public and receiving boxes of fan mail after being on the show for just a few months. From people looking genuinely confused about why 'Irene' was shopping at their local Woollies (and then being shocked to learn that her name was actually 'Lynne') to fans sending me deeply personal letters asking for advice that only Irene could give or relate to, it's curious to witness firsthand just how real *Home and Away* is to some viewers.

For a show that covers heavy themes such as infant loss, rape, sexual abuse, and alcoholism (to name just a few), I used to wonder why people were drawn to it when they could have been watching an uplifting romcom or easy-to-digest cooking show. (No pun intended.) But over the years, the abundance of fan mail we've received makes it clear. People relate. They relate to fallible Irene, resilient Leah, soft-hearted Marilyn, blustering John, no-nonsense Alf and Roo the peacemaker. They relate to heartbreak and tragedy and the general highs and lows of life. While yes, some of the stories over the years have been pretty out-there, at the heart of the show is vulnerability, a trait that makes us human.

While today I'm much better about creating boundaries when out in public (and we no longer really receive paper fan mail), when I first went from stage actor to being in people's lounge rooms five nights a week, I inadvertently became an armchair expert and confessional booth. Young gay guys would come out to me in letters, children would write to me saying they were being abused and rape victims would tell me their harrowing stories. And by 'me' I mean Irene.

Even though Irene didn't share her backstory chronicling the abuse she experienced as a child until recently, the writers did a good job alluding to the fact that she had not walked an easy path. As the unofficial village listener, she inspires this need in people to reach out and tell her what's going on in their lives in the hope that she will somehow be able to fix it. Only issue: it wasn't Irene reading the letters. It was me and I'm no life expert. Nor am I a psychologist. While I aim to be warm, encouraging and supportive, the truth is I'm not equipped to give mental health advice.

I would always write back and try to impart some sort of wisdom, but at the end of the day, all I could really do was refer them to crisis hotlines or tell them to speak to a teacher, parent, another trusted adult, or even the police. I know many other actors on the show over the years reacted in the same way.

Eventually the paper fan mail was stopped, partly due to the dead bird Tammin received but also because of an avalanche of abusive letters, suggestive photos and, in one case, a stack of papers with the C-word written everywhere. For many years the producers actually vetted our mail, but as everyone shifted to life online, fans started reaching out on message boards and through social media (which makes it a whole lot harder to screen the crazies!).

One of the most surprising letters I received was from former AFL star Ben Cousins. I can't remember exactly how it reached me, but one way or another I ended up sitting on my lounge reading about about Ben's struggles with being in and out of jail, addiction and his quest for a sense of self. During one stay in hospital, he started watching TV again and, in particular, *Home and Away*. He developed empathy for some of the characters, in particular Irene. He'd also seen me speak about the late Belinda Emmett while I was filming *Ladies' Night*. I'm no addiction counsellor, but I wrote back to Ben and offered him support and encouragement. Even though I never really understood his reasons for writing, it's an example of the impact characters on a long-running show can have.

I often wonder why so many people seem to relate to Irene. (I know it's not because she's good in bed because #funtriviafact – Irene doesn't have a bedroom.) Perhaps it's because she's had so much life thrown at her. Thanks to the amazing stable of writers over the years, she's overcome addiction, relapsed, overcome addiction again, salvaged relationships, forged lifelong friendships and found her happy place in the Bay.

The writers have allowed her to be vulnerable and resilient yet flawed. The producers and directors often encourage the actors, including me, to grab the baton and run with it, permitting us to hone a character, which the writers in turn will send out into the world on another journey. It sounds kind of wanky when I read this back, but it's the only way to describe it. I suppose it's why they're the writers and I'm the actor. With so much respect and gratitude to these extraordinary people who are micromanaging up to twenty-five Summer Bay lives at a time, I've been able to help create a character who pretty much loves unconditionally, rarely holds a grudge, and has had more hairstyles than hot dinners. (And whose fashion sense has improved beyond belief.)

As I say, some people love Irene, some people hate her, but very few people are indifferent. While I love getting the kind messages and requests for photo ops, I don't take offence when people let me know in no uncertain terms that they don't like me. Once, while at the airport on our way to Italy for Ada Nicodemou's fortieth birthday, a guy approached me. Figuring he wanted an autograph, I started rummaging around in my bag for a pen.

'Hi, you play Irene on *Home and Away*,' he stated, clearly looking for confirmation.

I smiled and nodded. 'Yep, that's me!'

'Your character just shits me beyond belief,' he said before walking off.

'And you have a nice day too, mate.'

Talk about a reality check.

Around my third year on the show, Irene went from a chain-smoking, platinum-blonde alcoholic to a tobacco-free, reformed and sober brunette/redhead. The smoking actually ended in the first three months of me portraying her because the producers wanted her to be liked and redeemed from the venom-spitting piece of work that she was when the public first met her. Believing that 'good people don't smoke', they had Sally catch Irene having a puff while pegging out sheets at the caravan park and saying, 'Smoking will *kill* you, Irene.'

And just like that, Irene gave up the ciggies. (Sadly, it wasn't that easy for Lynne.) The drastic hair change was due to the fact that I was pregnant! With Clancy now five, Paul and I were keen to keep our family growing and had been trying for a baby. When I finally received confirmation from a home pregnancy test (and the reappearance of those gorilla-like nipples), I told the producers my news and expressed my concerns about the weekly exposure to peroxide. While they were happy to accommodate my needs and were thrilled that I was expecting, they took full advantage of being able to write these changes into the show. First things first, Marilyn would dye Irene's hair brown.

Easy. Next they had to figure out what to do with my growing belly.

For some actors, it's a cinch getting creative with camera angles, or hiding behind coffee machines in the diner, or carrying boxes around for six months in order to conceal a pregnancy. But for me – someone who looks pregnant in the face, arms, boobs, back and fingernails – it was decided they'd write it into Irene's storyline by having her be a surrogate for Finlay's baby.

Having my pregnancy out in the open was exciting both on set and at home. Clancy was so chuffed about becoming a big sister and couldn't keep her little hands and ears off my tummy. Now that she was at school, Paul and I were aware of just how quickly kids grow up and were looking forward to reliving the adorable baby stage. (Even if that meant sleepless nights and incontinence.) Since I was now forty-three and, of course, having another 'geriatric pregnancy', I was a little more anxious about making it past the first trimester. But luckily, twelve weeks came and went and I relished the early stages of the cruisy second trimester.

At sixteen weeks, I even had the energy to attend a performance of *The Rocky Horror Picture Show* at Her Majesty's Theatre. I made it to 'The Time Warp' before having to pee for the one millionth time that day. While sitting on the toilet, I was baffled to see something hanging out of me that closely resembled a blood-soaked tampon string. I momentarily wondered if it was my umbilical cord. I wiped and it disappeared.

Hoping it was just spotting, and desperate not to lose hope, I decided not to say anything – in case it made it real. Subconsciously, I also began replaying all the miracle baby stories I'd heard over the years to reassure myself everything was fine.

Deep down though I knew something was wrong.

The following day I finished filming and then went straight to Clancy's school for a parent–teacher meeting. While sitting on a bench in the playground waiting for my turn, I was feeling hopeful that I hadn't had any more bleeding. I had an OB-GYN appointment lined up for the next day and knew I would get some answers soon. As I watched parents pop in and out of classrooms and wondered what Clancy's teacher was going to say, I suddenly felt my waters break. Devastated, I drove straight home.

'I don't think things are right,' I said to Paul through tears.

He held me and told me that whatever happened, we'd get through it.

The next day at my OB-GYN appointment, I went in already knowing the outcome. While I needed to hear the words from my doctor, I think I also needed a hug. Instead I got an apathetic bloke who put the ultrasound wand on my stomach and told me bluntly, 'There's nothing there anymore.' He then went on to say I'd had a 'spontaneous miscarriage' and that my baby had 'self-aborted'.

These words ricocheted around my head like bullets.

I drove home feeling numb. When I walked in the house, the look on my face confirmed what Paul suspected. The worst part was having to tell Clancy. Together, we all just held each other and cried at what could have been.

The day after that I had to miss work to have a D&C. In recovery, I couldn't help feeling like this was somehow God's way of punishing me for having an abortion at seventeen. An eye for an eye, right? But as my hormones levelled out, I got a bit more logical. I most likely lost the baby because I was forty-three.

My friend Susan, the first assistant director on *Home and Away*, was so sympathetic and held my hand both literally and figuratively through the process of trying to figure out what to do with Irene's pregnancy. Should she continue and give birth? Or should she miscarry like I had? One scenario would involve me having to go through the pregnancy I desperately wished I still had while the other would force me to relive the trauma of losing my baby. Trying to keep my head up and not derail the show, I decided to stay the course.

Irene would have Finlay's baby.

I can tell you from personal experience that the last thing a woman who's just experienced infant loss needs is a fake stomach strapped to her body. She also shouldn't be shown sonogram images of healthy foetuses. With the heat from the set lights beating down on my shoulders, I unfurled the black and white image of a baby in utero and completely broke down. Susan called for everyone to take a break and give me a moment.

This was to be expected, right? I had bottled up my heartbreak, my anger and my exhaustion and tried to bypass grief. Over the next ten minutes, I sobbed. I caught my breath. I stared at the sonogram. I gave myself permission to feel all the feelings. And then I called everyone back. By the time we got to the episode where Irene needed to give birth, the trauma had subsided and I was able to get through a very physical labour and delivery performance without having another breakdown.

Even though I was given a choice about what would happen

to Irene, I think deep down I just wanted to please everyone. There also wasn't really any scenario that was better than the other. I wanted to be fine and thought I could fake it. Turns out I wasn't and I couldn't. In hindsight, this was a big life lesson that it's okay to speak up. Thankfully, I had wonderful support and compassion from Paul, my family and my colleagues. While it's true that a lot of people don't know what to say in these sorts of situations, Debra Lawrance, who played Pippa, said something I still hold in my heart today. 'The baby got the wrong map.'

Sometimes things don't go right and that's okay too.

CHAPTER 12
The Murky Depths

I know what you're thinking.

You want to know the dirty bits.

I get it – you're human. I often wonder the same thing about the cast members of *Antiques Roadshow*. While I'd love to tell you all about the hook-ups that happen both on and off-screen, it's just not my style. I will, however, tell you about some of my favourite *Home and Away* filming hiccups. I'll dish the dirt on some truly bizarre fan fails. And yes, you bet, we will plumb the murky depths of ... the Logies.

But first, bear with me while I try to explain the complicated game of maintaining 'continuity' on a soap opera. First, you need to know that a 'Block' is a set of five episodes, which equates to one week's worth of shows. We identify these numerically. (For example, Block 24, Block 25, and so on.)

Next, you need to know that we film all the *exterior* scenes of a Block during one week and the *interior* scenes of the same Block the following week. Still with me? The exterior scenes are usually done 'on location', somewhere nice like Avalon, Palm Beach or the surprisingly filmic Kenthurst in Sydney's Hills district.

The interior scenes, which we refer to as 'in studio', are filmed in a building in the city. More on that later.

Finally, you need to know that we film the on location scenes of Block 25 while filming the in studio scenes of Block 24. The following week we film the on location scenes of Block 26 while filming the in studio scenes of Block 25. Confusing? Stay with me, people!

The upshot is when you see me walking into the diner in an episode, I don't actually film what happened inside until a week later.

This is where continuity comes into play.

Let's say you see me enter the diner with my hair in a ponytail and a brown handbag hanging from my shoulder. But then, all of a sudden, my hair is down and I'm bagless. To make it even weirder, my previously untucked green shirt is now tucked in ... and pink! You might think a long period of time has gone by. You might think I was suffering an identity crisis ... It doesn't matter what you're thinking, the issue is that your mind is yanked from the story and you start questioning things.

How can you possibly get your head around *another* murder or earthquake in Summer Bay when Irene's shirt just changed colour before your eyes?

On top of having a director and assistant director, we have a dedicated continuity person to ensure each cast member has the exact same hair, make-up, clothing and props in each Block. This is crucial to maintaining the believability of the show. For the most part, this way of filming goes off without a hitch. The only exceptions are if an actor is sick or injured, if there's a pandemic or when the Christmas break rolls around.

Due to our filming schedule, every year we end up filming the on location scenes of the new Block 1 while filming in studio scenes of the old Block 46 before we break for the holidays. Four weeks later, we come back and film the in studio scenes for Block 1 (while filming on location scenes for Block 2). Turns out, a *lot* can change in a four-week period. We all have that one Cypriot friend (I'm talking about you, Ada Nicodemou) who goes to the beach on the first day of the summer holidays and instantly changes nationalities. While I haven't been blessed with that type of skin, I am keenly aware that in the span of four weeks, my body is more than happy to latch onto any pavlova or pinot noir that floats my way. Due to that fact, I'm conscious to stay healthy during the break.

Apparently, so was Daniel Amalm.

In 1994, Daniel came on the show to portray Jack Wilson, the foster son of Pippa and Michael. Daniel was great fun and showed real potential. You could just tell that he was going to be successful in whatever he pursued. He was also a budding musician and clearly talented. At this stage, he was what you might call a stocky build.

Anyway, after filming the on location scenes of Block 1, we broke for our annual four-week holiday. Evidently, Daniel thought this would be a fantastic time to up his fitness regime. Unlike removing weight from a post-menopausal woman, the kilos *fell* off Daniel and he came back 10 kilograms lighter and ripped (as the kids would say).

Uh oh.

As previously mentioned, anything that is out of continuity stands out like dogs' balls on screen. For a week, fans had to watch Daniel go from Chunky Monkey on the streets of Palm Beach to SAS Body inside the diner. I'm not kidding, he became so chiselled that in some scenes he had the jawline of Arnold

Schwarzenegger and others he was like a teddy bear who had just had its wisdom teeth removed.

Given that Paul reads my contracts for me, I can't be entirely sure, but I feel like somewhere in there it says: don't dramatically change your appearance without *Home and Away*'s permission. Reshooting scenes takes a lot of time and effort. And money. From memory, we've only had to do it once and it was when a quite well-known actor forgot they'd already shot on location scenes and cut their hair short. They had to film the exterior scenes again because it was honestly like watching Lady Godiva hair breeze into a building and then Judy Dench's noggin greet you hello.

Filming out of order can really make your head spin. It's much easier to maintain your commitment to an emotion when you're on a roll and going with the natural progression of a conversation or movement. That's one of the great things about the theatre. But on TV, you're always going to someone's funeral *before* they die, or having life-saving surgery *before* you have your heart attack! But that just comes with the territory.

You know what else comes with the territory?

Busloads of fans.

I'm talking about actual busloads. Pre-COVID, there was a business that used to take people from Sydney to Palm Beach to watch us film. For a while we would all do our best to facilitate meet-and-greets, but thanks to the pandemic and the need to socially distance, we had to take a step back. In a way we were kind of grateful for it because on a forty-degree day, after spending ten hours waiting to capture five minutes of film, the last thing you want to do is feel beholden to take a photo with someone who has just elbowed their way (literally) to the front of the line.

Most fans are lovely, but there are always those pushy few who seem to have left Marjorie Manners at home. As I'd give a chummy smile and wait for the click of a camera, I'd always think, 'A "please" wouldn't go astray!'

Besides the pushy types, I used to be really judgmental of the truly weird fans. But in 2011, something happened that forever changed the way I understand the concept of 'star struck'.

The talent show *The X Factor* had just come to Australia. As *Home and Away* is a Channel 7 stable mate, we all got on board for the launch. While wandering around the room, I took a sip of bubbles before noticing Spice Girl Mel B standing right across from me. I decided to officially welcome her to Australia. (In my head I imagined she'd think I was *such* a hospitable person, want to become best friends with me, then come to my house so I could introduce her to Clancy, and then we'd all live happily ever after ...)

As I entered Mel's line of sight, she smiled and said, 'Hello.'

I confidently stretched out my hand and said, 'Hi, I'm Mel.'

Then I added, 'No I'm not. *You're* Mel. I'm Lynne!'

A wave of shame and embarrassment washed over me. I instantly realised I was not going to be capable of stringing any sort of meaningful sentence together so I aborted my mission. I mumbled, 'I'm going,' before turning and walking away.

Scary Spice must have thought I was off my meds.

This interaction made me realise how easy it is for us all to do silly things and behave in bizarre ways. I had genuinely wanted to be so cool and calm, but my body demanded that I word-vomit before slinking away like a moron. Now when people are a little awkward around me, I always think of the Great Mel B Fail of 2011. Thankfully, I did have a chance to redeem myself (sort of) when in England a few years later. I introduced myself to another Spice Girl, Mel C, and was able to identify myself correctly.

In my thirty years as a TV actress, probably the weirdest fan interaction I ever witnessed had nothing to do with me. In 2019, Paul and I were in the UK for both business and pleasure. I was scheduled to appear on a morning show for a *Home and Away* interview. When we got to the studio and were walking along the corridors, we spotted the comedian and fellow Australian Adam Hills, who was there to host his show, *The Last Leg*. Adam must have recognised me because he made a point of coming over and saying hello. Before I could even begin to introduce Paul, I saw a hand reach out and touch Adam's face.

It was Paul's hand. And it was clutching beard hair.

'How do you get your beard so nice and soft?'

These very words came from Paul's mouth.

As I watched Adam process the fact that a stranger had literally just stroked his beard without consent, part of me died and will forever lie in rest in the corridor of that building. I tried to form words in an effort to explain that Paul knew Adam had been growing his beard until Brexit was resolved and that it was a simple case of 'thinking you know a celebrity on a personal level when you totally don't', but it was too late.

Adam managed to not punch Paul. He offered a simple, 'I've got to get going ...' salutation before turning and quite literally running away.

Just last night I raised this little incident with my dearly beloved. What did he do? He tried to defend himself!

'It wasn't *that* bad. I just reached up and stroked it.'

I pleaded with him to stop using the word 'stroke' and to just admit he beard-handled Adam Hills.

This memorable-for-all-the-wrong-reasons encounter, however, gave me a lot of insight into the whole TV fan thing. When you see someone regularly on the telly, it's hard to remember that you don't actually know them and they don't know you, either. Just because you feel as though they understand you on a deeper level does not mean that they want anything to do with you.

They *especially* don't want you to touch them on the face. Or anywhere else, for that matter.

Believe it or not, Paul stroking Adam Hills' beard was not the most embarrassing moment of my life. (Most awkward – yes. Embarrassing – no.) To this day, I still have PTSD flashbacks from filming a diner scene at the old Channel 7 studios in Epping. This day started out like any other. I woke up early, drove to the set, spent an hour in hair and make-up, had a bit of morning tea, ran through some lines and then entered the diner to begin filming. This was during the late 1990s when the diner still had booths.

While doing my blocking that required me to bend over and pick up a napkin from the depths of a booth bench seat (a challenge to say the least), I let out what can only be described as the fart that was heard around the Bay. (It was one of those real trumpety ones.) Startled by the number of decibels I had created suddenly – there was only silence. Crickets.

Not knowing how to handle the situation, I placed my hands on my heart and simply said, 'I'm so sorry, everybody.'

The crew burst into laughter. A cameraman said, 'We didn't think it was you! We thought it was one of us or an extra.'

I had just confessed to farting publicly and no one even knew it had been me!

Or maybe they did know, but when it comes to old ladies passing wind, you just smile and pretend like nothing happened.

Impromptu farting aside, getting to live life on a soap is incredibly good fun. Being part of the Channel 7 family means getting to grow my network of friends in a way I don't think I could have done if I had stuck to theatre. Over the years, I've been able to go to numerous awards shows, which of course always include the Logies. Attending Australian television's 'night of nights' is a bit like running a marathon in terms of preparations and endurance. The day is long and arduous and unless you're born with the ability to maintain perfect make-up and stand in heels for ten hours, it takes considerable mental strength. Even though I love the people I get to meet and catch up with, it is one of my least favourite physical activities.

I've attended about twenty-five Logie ceremonies so far. I don't naturally gravitate towards diamantes and eight-inch heels, so I spent the first fifteen of those needing a *little* extra help to get through the day (if you catch my drift). And I definitely wasn't the only one. The only year I behaved myself was when I was asked to prepare a speech in case *Home and Away* won.

And in case you're wondering, we did win! In fact, we're the most successful soap in Logies history. It meant a lot to me when I was asked to give our acceptance speech in 2016 because I got the chance to thank all of the important people who make my job so damn gratifying and a show I'm so proud to be on. From the ladies in the Channel 7 canteen to the guys on the scaffolding outside the building, I was determined to not overlook a soul.

Okay, it was a longish speech, but *Home and Away* has managed to attract and retain some truly awesome humans. Take, for example, Carol Toohey, who was our studio cook at the time. Carol made all the food for the diner, Alf's dinner table and pretty much anything anyone else ate on screen. She also kept the cast and crew's energy levels up on long days by bringing us plates of delicious cheese toasties. You get my point. This woman was (and still is) a total queen and I was determined to thank her – along with all the other fabulous cast members, crew, office workers, directors and producers.

However – and I only found this out later – just seconds into my speech, Channel 9 saw fit to cut to a bunch of commercials. Bugger me! So while the people in the room heard the entire spiel, the people at home only heard, 'Thank you so much for this award. On behalf of the cast, I'd like to thank *TV Week* ...' (And cut!)

Thankfully, Cameron Welsh, our producer, put out a memo informing all the underwhelmed crew who hadn't been in the room on the night that I had indeed thanked every last one of them and not been struck down with a bizarre, out-of-character reticence.

Back in the day, *TV Week* would decide the winners by sending out ballots that people could fill out and mail in. It was like this pure fan-driven competition that felt really authentic. But now, actors who are nominated go out and promote themselves on social media. Relentlessly. I know I sound old school, but honestly, I die when I see people post 'Vote for Me!' under a duck-face selfie.

Obviously, if any of my cast-mate friends are nominated I would rally my social media troops to vote for them. But not if they were doing the 'Vote for Me!' duck-face thing. Which they wouldn't because they have an embarrassment gland, unlike some of these new kids on the block.

Maybe I'm just secretly grumpy because I've never been nominated personally for a Logie (let alone a gold one), but I just think people need to be a bit more humble about receiving awards. (The irony of me venting about this in my *celebrity memoir* is not lost on me.) #buymybook #voteforme #makemeabestseller

CHAPTER 13
Thank You, St Jude (and Coral)

Have you ever wanted something so badly that you found yourself praying to God, every saint you can think of, Buddha and any other deity in the universe that can hear you? I'm talking about the kind of obsession that makes you spend your weekly grocery money on a stack of magazines so you can carefully craft a vision board in an effort to somehow manifest your dream. (You might even consider dropping $5000 to attend a Tony Robbins event to gain the personal development habits needed to attain it.)

If you answered 'yes' then me too! In the early 1990s, I fell head over heels in love with the idea of doing pantomime overseas. 'Panto' as we call it in the biz seemed to combine most of my favourite things in life: the UK, comedy, singing, acting, and being completely and utterly ridiculous. Just like when you're thinking about buying a new car and you start seeing the same make and model everywhere, from the moment the panto idea entered my head, it seemed like everyone was doing it. Actors like Jackie Woodburne, Ian Smith, Kate Ritchie, Rebekah Elmaloglou, Anne Charleston and of course our own Ray Meagher would fly over every Christmas season to bring a classic fairy tale to life.

While the word on the street was that they were all making vast sums of money, I was mostly envious that they got to be onstage singing, dancing and acting up. Even though the idea of being a cashed-up panto performer was enticing, I truly didn't want to do it for the money. (Which was a good thing because by the time I joined in on the fun in the mid-1990s, the hype of Aussie soap had died down along with the size of the pay packet.)

Determined to join the throng, I asked my agent, Joolee Eadie, to see what she could do. Next, I added St Jude to my list of higher powers to pray to because when I had been reading the paper, I kept noticing numerous 'Thank you, St Jude' personal ads. Curious, I investigated St Jude and learnt that he was the Patron Saint of Desperate Cases and Lost Causes. The deal is:

once you pray to him and have your prayers answered, you need to publish your gratitude. (True, I'm not a Catholic, but figured it wouldn't hurt to have all hands on deck.)

While I would like to think it was the fact that I had worn my knees raw while praying, it was more likely Joolee's connection to Simon Barry of New Pantomime Productions that opened the door for me. In 1995, I was offered the role of Fairy Bowbells in *Dick Whittington*, published my gratitude for St Jude in the *Herald* and was given nine weeks off to go to the UK that December.

I was astonished I didn't have to audition. I suppose it was because both *Home and Away* and *Neighbours* were really big over there and the producers could watch our ability to 'over act' from the comfort of their own homes. Clancy was just about to turn five, which made the idea of a twenty-four-hour flight feel like a Herculean task. Luckily, she has always been a pretty good traveller and at this point in my life, I was able to contort myself into positions conducive to sleep in an economy seat.

Getting some sort of rest was crucial because on the very day we landed, I had to go to a read-through with the rest of the cast. The show was being held at the Brighton Dome, which meant that after our twenty-four-hour flight, we jumped on a train and travelled another hour south to our pre-arranged apartment. By the time we got there and dropped our bags, we must have looked like a post-apocalyptic zombie family. (If in this post-apocalyptic world, said zombie family lived in the most flamboyant and ornate one-bedroom home you can imagine.) I'm talking red velvet floor-to-ceiling curtains, gold fixtures that glistened like a stripper's belly button and the type of suggestive artwork that makes you instinctively tell curious small children to look away.

Basically, the flat resembled Robin Williams' Miami home in *The Birdcage*.

Ray and Rupert, the wonderful and generous gay couple who owned the place, can take full credit for the opulence. With my head feeling like it had gone through a tumble dryer and a migraine being triggered by the abundance of iridescent decor, I gave strict instructions to Paul and Clancy before heading out for the read-through.

'Whatever you do, don't touch or break anything. But most importantly – do *not* fall asleep.'

'We won't,' Paul said while exploring what would be our new home for the next eight weeks.

'I'm serious. I don't have a key and you'll need to let me back in. I also don't want to be kept awake by a wired child all night.'

Paul looked a bit absentminded.

'What are you looking at?' I asked as I followed him into the flat's small glass conservatory. It was decorated with ornate pots filled with yonic lilies, wrought-iron chairs (that you just know would leave the worst imprint on the back of your thighs) and a glass coffee table I definitely didn't want Clancy to go anywhere near. Then I saw what had caught Paul's attention. In the corner was a life-size china figurine of a fawn-coloured (which is a nice way of saying 'orange') Afghan hound.

I looked at Clancy whose mind would no doubt be teeming with wild four-year-old ideas.

'And definitely *don't* touch that,' I said with my arms akimbo.

Even though I was off my scone and extremely jet-lagged, I made it through the read-through. In fact, everything went swimmingly and I was feeling confident to be back on an actual theatre stage! There was only one issue. I was told I'd need to frequently teeter on the Dome's passerelle, which is a tiny metre-wide walkway that divided the audience, orchestra and stage. This would have been fine except for the fact that I'd be wearing my voluminous Fairy Bowbells costume.

Fifty shades of pink and boasting more tulle than all of the ballerina costumes in the world combined, my outfit's skirt stuck out so wide (thanks to a very sturdy and unbendable hoop) that I had to flip it to be parallel to my body to go through doorways. Since it prevented me from seeing my feet, walking on the passerelle felt a bit like walking on a tightrope over a river of crocodiles – blindfolded.

Okay, so I wasn't at risk of falling into the jaws of a hungry reptile, but I might have easily toppled into a tuba or got a drumstick jammed somewhere no drumstick should ever be jammed. I couldn't see the musicians at all. (God only knows what *they* saw.) Even though I was now petrified I was going to suffer a very public and very mortifying fall dressed as a damn fairy, I walked the two kilometres back to the flat feeling grateful and borderline giddy about how much fun I was going to have.

My daydreaming was interrupted when I realised I hadn't actually taken note of which flat was ours. Since this was the time before mobile phones, I was left to peer through lit windows and will myself to recognise front stoops and door knobs. Finally feeling confident that I had the right one, I knocked and knocked and knocked.

Nothing.

Desperate to swan dive into the oasis of satin sheets I'd spied on our bed just hours earlier, I wedged my way behind a prickly hedge and started tapping on the window. That's when I saw Paul and Clancy blissfully asleep on the lounge. Since they were clearly in the stage of sleep that borders on comatose, I had to perpetuate every 'bloody mad Australian woman' stereotype and use an extra loud 'Oi, Paul! Wake up, ya bastard!' as I continued to rap on the window. Finally he woke up and let me in. Even though I was completely beside myself from this half-hour ordeal, I decided I wouldn't divorce him. (Mostly because we weren't actually married and I couldn't.)

Once our heads were screwed back on and we no longer fell asleep at 6 p.m. each night, it didn't take us too long to find our groove in Brighton, which might very well be where the term 'camp' was invented. This place has one of the best gay and lesbian communities I've ever had the pleasure of living among. A very kind couple at the local pub, the Black Horse (aka the Pink Pony), then owned by our still dear friends, Bill and Tony, took Clancy under their wing and taught her how to play pool.

When she wasn't busy winning the hearts of the locals, she got asked to be one of the 'tinies' in the show. This meant she got to perform in her own adorable little outfit alongside her mum! I remember the first night she walked out onstage, her knees were literally knocking with fear. I was also nervous. Not because of performing for the public, but because the opening night's audience was loud. My initial thoughts were, *Wow, these poms really love their Aussie soap stars*. Sadly, it wasn't my presence that was eliciting all the chanting and hollering. It was due to the fact that a performer from a popular British reality TV show was in our cast.

Instead of soap-loving families coming to watch their children's eyes light up with wonder and glee, we had a roomful of rambunctious reality TV fans. I'm not going to lie, I got the shits real quick. Not only because this guy had no sense of ensemble and was oblivious to the fact that there were children around, but because he seemed convinced he was the only star turn. (He wasn't.) He would constantly pull focus from the other actors while onstage by making silly gestures and essentially distracting the audience.

It was one thing when he did it to me (annoying, but I was big enough and ugly enough to pull focus right back), but it was quite another when he did it to the legendary Frank Williams. Dear old Frank was myopic to the point of nearly being legally blind. To know this man is to love him and his talent is enormous. (Any *Dad's Army* fans out there?) As someone who felt like I had enough experience and credibility to say something, I kindly told our reality TV star and a few other 'newbies' how important it was not to upstage the other actors when it's their line or song. In fact, I urged, 'We need to actively give them focus.'

Well, the following night I watched our reality TV star act like a buffoon and completely diminish Frank's performance yet again. As Frank did his best to soldier on, my body took note of the Red Mist finding its way from Summer Bay to Brighton. The curtain had barely hit the boards before I marched over and spat, 'You're a real piece of work! How dare you show such disrespect!'

Since he towered over me at six foot four, which essentially put my eyes in line with his stomach, I can't tell you what his facial expression was. But I do remember him remaining silent and feeling like he'd absorbed what I'd said. With that, I stormed off. (Which wasn't as cool as it should have been due to my ridiculous tutu knocking over props and small children on the way.)

Yet again, I'd publicly allowed the Red Mist to coat my words. At least this time it wasn't in defence of myself. When someone like Frank Williams is being blatantly disrespected, I just can't help myself. Afterwards, Frank pulled me aside and said in his unmistakable English accent, 'Thank you, darling, thank you.'

I must say that having a douchebag panto cast member and an out-of-control audience was not typical. For the most part, everyone involved brought professionalism, wit, charm and talent. Even the audience was known for being interactive and gracious. However, every now and then, the Dome was full of pensioners who'd fall asleep the minute they sat down or sit stony-faced as it was clear they'd been dragged there against their will. Our wonderful musical director, Chris Hocking, would stand in the orchestra and use his booming cockney voice to cheer us on or defend our honour. 'Don't worry about 'em, darlin'! They're all deaf and stupid anyway!' he'd yell. (I love it when a boss doesn't abide by 'the customer is always right' adage.)

Speaking of deaf audiences ...

After performing in Brighton for five weeks and experiencing our first white Christmas, we took the show on the road to Widnes in Cheshire, which is famous for being where Sporty Spice was raised and, more importantly, where Paul Simon wrote 'Homeward Bound'. I don't want this to sound negative, but back then in Widnes, the abundance of smoke stacks combined with the lack of an actual theatre in which to perform made us miss Brighton terribly.

And yet the show must go on ... even if it's in a scout hall.

Suddenly our professional production felt more like a group of kids performing a Christmas concert at an underfunded showground. We didn't have dressing rooms and the stage manager only had one arm, which wouldn't have been an issue, but being a scout hall, there were no hydraulics, no fly system, no nothing really, so the poor bloke had to run across the stage dragging the curtain behind him. More than once he fell head first while just trying to do his job. The upside was that the audience thought it was part of the act! With the foldable chairs packed full of pensioners who appeared to have narcolepsy, we enthusiastically sang and danced ... apparently to just amuse ourselves.

To make it even more one-sided, there were rarely any kids

in the audience. When I went to do the obligatory Q&A and singsong at the end of the show with a child, I had to use Clancy.

'And what's your name, little girl?' I cooed.

'Clancy!' she excitedly answered now that she was a bit more used to being onstage.

'And why are you here tonight?' I hoped she'd say something that would garner at least an 'aw' from the lacklustre crowd.

'Uh ... you made me!' she said.

Silence. Even after I turned her blunt response into what I deemed a clever joke, I got nothing but a cough from an elderly man in the front row. I'm not exaggerating ... the one-armed stage manager falling over while opening the curtain got more of a reaction. (Now that I think about it, maybe he was doing it deliberately.)

When the show finally ended, I ran offstage with the other cast members. As I caught my breath, I just couldn't help myself. 'They're all effing *dead*,' I said laughing. That's when I saw the sound technician leap from behind his pile of cords onto the stage and sprint at us yelling, 'Your microphone's still on!'

Whoops. I doubt they could hear me anyway.

When cast in a panto production, you're usually committed to doing between eight and sixteen shows a week for approximately six weeks. Even though I never feel more alive and stimulated than when I'm onstage, over the years I've noticed that after delivering the same lines and gags roughly twenty times, I get kind of bored and a little stir-crazy. When I mention this to people, they're stunned and always ask me how on earth I've stayed on *Home and Away* for nearly thirty years. My answer: Irene is living a life and no two days in the Bay are ever the same.

Because Irene is an empath who fiercely strives to protect her relationships, it's hard to get bored with her character. I truly feel like I can apply to my own life so much of the advice she delivers on the show. (On the off-chance I ever need to deter a teen from joining a cult or help one of my friends from falling down a sinkhole ...)

However, with so many different people's storylines happening at once, it's not surprising when your role takes a back seat. Occasionally this makes some of the younger actors anxious because they're worried they'll be written out of the show. Other times they just want more airtime. Regardless of the reason, whenever they felt stagnant or that their characters weren't doing enough, I'd watch them make an appointment with the writers, walk upstairs and ask what was in store.

Since the writers are warm and receptive and always happy to hear our ideas, they'd usually take the hint that they needed to spice up someone's storyline. And just like that, a major drama would go down in Summer Bay. As an older actor who had to go through menopause on set, I didn't mind having a bit of downtime. (You try not visibly sweating through Irene's aka the Nylon Queen's clothing under film set lights after drinking hot coffee and having your hair blow-dried.) Needless to say, the fact that Irene gravitated towards being a sounding board, hugger and caregiver was fine with me ... until recently.

Shortly after celebrating my twenty-seventh anniversary on the show, I started to feel like I hadn't been pushed out of my comfort zone for a while. Taking a page out of my co-stars' playbook, I made an appointment and took the walk upstairs to meet with the writers. Boom. Within two weeks, Irene had stumbled upon her charge, Bella Nixon, about to be sexually assaulted by a man who had been grooming her online. In a fit of rage and fuelled by her own childhood trauma, Irene nearly kills the bloke with a lamp.

After the attack, I spent fourteen hours a day over the next three months filming the most physically and emotionally demanding *Home and Away* scenes I've ever done. While it was absolutely amazing and gratifying to dig deep and bring the scenes to life, that was the last time I'll ever walk up those stairs to see the writers!

I feel incredibly blessed to say that I've blissfully gone to work every day feeling confident, proud and, all in all, secure in my job. That is until 2019 when I was being interviewed by radio stars Jonesy and Amanda on WSFM. As far as interviews go, I always love talking to these guys because they're clever, funny and incredibly decent human beings. After decades of answering questions like, 'How does it feel to be the longest-running female cast member?' and 'Do you still love being on the show?' I knew this little chat could be had in my sleep. I think I might have been simultaneously cooking brekky while I chatted.

Completely out of the blue, Jonesy chimed in with, 'It's amazing to think that they nearly wrote you out in 2002.'

'I'm sorry, *what?*' (If I'd had a drink in my mouth, I'm confident that droplets would have been flying through the air.)

'Yeah, it's on Wikipedia.'

Apparently, there were plans to write Irene out because the producers felt like she didn't have anywhere to go now that her kids were gone. By a stroke of luck, a new script producer by the name of Coral Drouyn had arrived and was horrified. She pleaded with the producers to let me stay and said she had big plans for Irene. While you'd think I would have picked up on this at work through green room chatter, this was literally the first I had heard of it.

As soon as the interview was over, I immediately found Paul and told him that a woman named Coral had saved my bacon back in 2002! To be honest, I think I'm still digesting this news because of how much of a shock it was. I know 'job security' and 'actor' aren't two things you typically associate with each other, but my *Home and Away* 'family' is just that – a group of people who have enriched my life tremendously, taught me so many valuable lessons, given me some of my most cherished memories and yielded some truly wonderful friendships.

CHAPTER 14
A Reason and a Lifetime

After *Dick Whittington* wrapped, I made going back to the UK a nearly annual tradition. Over the years, I've had the pleasure of doing numerous performances of *Jack and the Beanstalk*, *Aladdin*, *Cinderella*, *Snow White* and *Beauty and the Beast*. While my fellow actors, the sets, the costumes, the songs and being onstage with my daughter Clancy are some of my most vivid memories, what I cherish most from my time doing panto are the lifelong friendships I made along the way.

I believe that people come into your life for a reason, a season or a lifetime. During our early years in England, we made friends we've kept for both a reason *and* a lifetime. When performing in *Aladdin* in Ashton-under-Lyne near Manchester, I was working with an actor by the name of James Crossley. A lovely chap, we had a scheduled break and went to visit mutual friends in York.

James had a best mate named Garth in York whose parents, Maureen and Phil, happened to own the Judge's Lodgings, where we stayed at a heavily discounted rate. Built in the 1700s, this stunning boutique hotel set the scene for long talks over wine, the type of joke telling that results in snort-laughter and the start of one of my dearest friendships.

For reasons that can't really be pinpointed (pheromones? love of the same cultural references? shared appreciation for fermented grapes?), there are some people in life that you just hit it off with. For me, that was Maureen (whom most call Maudy) and Phil. They exude a warmth that makes you feel like everything is going to be okay. On top of being up for any adventure, they're the type of friends you can comfortably sit with in silence. Our families spent decades bonding over the universal ups and downs of life and making wonderful memories. When Maudy and Phil would visit us in Australia, they got to know my family and friends. When Paul and I would visit the UK, we got to know their kids, Nicky and Garth, as well as their families.

In 2010, things got really difficult for Maudy. A heavy

smoker, she'd fallen ill with a terrible lung infection that required hospitalisation. Frantic that she was going to die, I made plans to fly over. Before I could purchase my ticket, Phil called to tell me that she had just had a portion of her lung removed in surgery and was going to be okay. He also mentioned that while she was being operated on, their daughter Nicky discovered at her own doctor's appointment that she had breast cancer. That year happened to be Maudy's sixtieth, Nicky's fortieth and her eldest son Jack's eighteenth. Over the next nine years, I witnessed my friend watch her daughter fight as hard as she could. I also witnessed Nicky squeeze every last drop out of life.

Around that time, in what best could be described as art imitating life, the *Home and Away* writers dropped a bomb: they told me that Irene was going to be diagnosed with breast cancer. Obviously, this was a topic very fresh in my mind (and heavy in my heart) so I was feeling particularly emotional about reading their ideas.

When our resident medical advisor, Wendy O'Donnell, began researching breast cancer and how we could accurately portray the experience, I opened up about Nicky's recent diagnosis. Wendy ended up writing to Nicky to find out more about her particular cancer, her treatment and the prognosis. As avid soap opera fans, both Nicky and Maudy religiously watched *Home and Away* (along with *EastEnders*, *Coronation Street* and *Emmerdale*).

Enthusiastic, happy to help, and excited to contribute to one of our storylines, Nicky sent through loads of information her doctors had offered her – including their recommendation she took a particular heart medication. Wendy and the writers decided to parallel the stories, which is why Irene is now on heart medication for the rest of her life. They also used Nicky's experience with mouth ulcers, extreme nausea, weight loss, hair loss and exhaustion to help Irene's battle feel more real. When Nicky went into remission, so did Irene.

Unfortunately, while Irene stayed in remission, Nicky did not.

After four years, Nicky's cancer returned, this time in her liver and brain. Just like the first time, this news did not stop her from living life to the fullest. (I truly believe that her use of marijuana oil prolonged her time and gave her a quality of life she might not have otherwise had.) Nicky seized every opportunity to spend time with her family, play with her friends, attend Robbie Williams concerts, laugh at a Michael McIntyre show and even come see me do a panto performance of *Beauty and the Beast* at the York Opera House during the 2017/2018 season. As I watched her refuse to let her cancer get in her way, I knew that while she still had breath in her lungs and movement in her body, she was going to do everything in her power to not die wondering.

I'm not the first person to have a close friend be diagnosed with cancer and I won't be the last, but I felt compelled to do something more. Since I was never going to find a cure for the disease myself, I figured the next best thing would be to raise awareness, which is why I decided to accept an offer to be part of Channel 7's TV special *The All New Monty: Ladies' Night*. Originally produced in the UK and inspired by the movie *The Full Monty*, Australia's live and televised *Ladies' Night* was essentially a group of ladies dancing and then showing their 'full monty' (aka boobies) in an effort to raise awareness about breast cancer and encourage women to get mammograms. (They were also simultaneously filming a revival of the men's version called *The Real Full Monty* with George Burgess, Matty J, Sam Moran, Lote Tuqiri, Robert DiPierdomenico, John Wood, Brendan Fevola and of course Todd McKenney in an effort to raise awareness for men's health.)

I was thrilled to be involved, but also more than slightly terrified at the idea of getting my puppies out in a room packed with people. I overcame this fear when I thought about how brave breast cancer fighters and survivors have to be on a daily basis. With *Home and Away*'s Georgie Parker as the host and Todd, whom I'd met while doing *Dancing with the Stars* (oh yes, we will get to that experience, don't you worry), doing the choreography, I felt like my soon-to-be-bared chest was in very good hands, so to speak.

Alongside Nadia Bartel, Simone Callahan, Lisa Curry, Casey

Donovan, Rachael Finch, Ella Hooper and Georgie, we spent weeks rehearsing and filming content for a live show and TV special. On top of learning our striptease choreography, we encouraged women shopping in Myer to have their breasts checked on the spot by wearing crazy wigs and talking in silly accents. Apparently in an Eastern European mood, I chose a long black wig and proceeded to put on a thick and very bad Russian accent while I led ladies to qualified health professionals.

Another fun activity involved getting our boobs painted for a charity calendar entitled So Brave. Unfortunately, I think I got the work experience girl who took about four days to paint me. I don't know if it was her attention to detail around my tiny nipples or the fact that I had slightly more excess skin than my co-stars, but I felt like I was never going to get out of that chair. (To this day I'm still finding glitter where no mature woman should ever have glitter.)

One day during filming, I was asked about Nicky. Even though Todd and Georgie had warned me the producers were going to ask me about her and I mentally steeled myself to maintain a brave face and speak passionately on behalf of my wild, wonderful and resilient friend, I still broke down. Nicky's plight was so dominant in my life at that point. Short of divine intervention, I knew that her time was finite, as she'd now been moved to a hospice. Surrounded by family, she was being lovingly cared for.

Part of me felt guilty and helpless that I wasn't in the UK with my dearest friend Maudy while she held her dying daughter's hand, but they both loved the idea of me raising awareness for breast cancer and if I left now, it would defeat the whole purpose.

The producers also asked me about Belinda Emmett. I'll never forget her telling us in the *Home and Away* make-up room back in 1998 that she'd found a lump in her breast. She was just twenty-three. Her sister had found a cyst in her breast and Belinda assumed that's all it was. Everyone present urged her to get it checked. It was breast cancer. After a seven-year battle, she tragically passed away in 2006, just shy of her thirtieth birthday.

A few weeks after talking to the producers, while taking a dance fit class with Clancy and her friends, I received a message from Maudy. Nicky was gone. As I stood there staring at the incomprehensible but not unexpected words, I felt my heart sink to my stomach. Grief and sadness can be so physical. I looked over at my young and vibrant daughter and felt compelled to hug her. How on earth had Maudy's daughter been taken? Why did two lovely kids have to lose such a caring and exuberant mother? Why did her doting husband have to lose his wife and best friend?

I left the class and immediately started texting Maudy. I let her know that I was there for her and for her to call me whenever she was ready to talk. As I sat there trying to figure out what to do next, I realised that I had been in this situation before. Except last time, Maudy was the person I turned to. While Nicky was in remission, I found out my dear friend Kerrie's son, Jayden, had been killed in an accident. He was only twenty.

Kerrie is a friend I have loved and considered a soulmate for over twenty years. Her husband Mark, Paul and I have dinner almost every week, travel together often and basically consider ourselves serial double daters. Clancy went to school with Kerrie's eldest son, Ryan, and Kerrie's littlest, Connor, played baby Olivia on *Home and Away*. (The show's youngest crossdresser to date.)

Kerrie's middle child, Jayden, was an avid pilot and had been doing solo flight training in Victoria when his plane went down. Frozen, I had to call Maudy to process what I'd just heard. We talked about how losing a parent is a terrible thing, how losing a friend or a sister or a brother is just as awful, but how there is something about losing a child – no matter what age you are or what age they are – that is almost unhealable. We agreed that all you can do is simply be there. With that, I sent Kerrie a text letting her know that I was there if she needed to talk, vent, scream, cry, or simply just sit in silence. She called at 1 a.m. the next morning.

I was humbled to be asked to write and deliver Jayden's eulogy. The church was heaving with family, friends, classmates and colleagues as we celebrated his love of cricket, his larrikin ways and his natural ability to make people laugh. We also talked about his passion for flying and how it was his true love in life.

As we listened to the minister speak in front of the huge glass windows, a plane flew overhead. It was most likely we were under a flight path, but for all of us there, we felt it was Jayden's seal of approval for a proper send-off.

After the funeral, I was entrusted with the job of picking up his ashes. I drove to the crematorium, reverently received him, strapped him into the car, and chatted with him the whole way home. While Jayden may no longer be in his body, I like to think he's still with us. He had always loved owls and one of the things that brings his family peace is that for months after his accident, an owl would fly down and sit on his parents' driveway. Often in the middle of the day.

When you receive this type of news about a friend, you might not know what to say, but you instinctively want to go to them. You want to hold them, cry with them, bring them cups of tea, maybe a vat of wine, and just be there. With Kerrie and Mark, it was easy for Paul and me to join the many people by their side because we all lived in the same town. But with Maudy, not only did I have an ocean to cross, I had contractual obligations which were proving very difficult to get out of.

With the *Ladies' Night*'s live performance slated for April (and the televised version due to air in September), not to mention my simultaneous filming of *Home and Away*, I was struggling to work out a way to get to the UK for Nicky's funeral. Maudy understood and knew that I would come as soon as I could. She also wanted to see *Ladies' Night* come to fruition, as it was something both she and Nicky were excited about. When it came time for the big night, it was one of the most emotional things I've ever done. Every single second, I thought about Nicky, Belinda and all the other brave women who have died from breast cancer. I thought about the fragility of life. I also considered how lucky I was to have all my family and most of my friends present.

While I may have left the stage feeling empowered and proud of the awareness we were raising, I was acutely aware that Clancy's boyfriend, Luke, had just seen his girlfriend's mum's boobs.

I'm sure he's still in therapy.

While we're on the topic of therapy, after the girls performed, the men took their turn. It was at this moment, in a theatre in Sydney, that I saw John Wood's doodle. I'll never un-see that. (I won't un-see Todd's either.) That said, I'm sure many people that night were also thinking, *Oh my God, I just saw Lynne McGranger's boobs. How do I un-see that?*

CHAPTER 15
Hatches, Matches and Dispatches

As you may recall from earlier chapters, I consistently went to church in my youth (for the boys and collection plate money), sporadically in my young adult life (to get married and regret it), and then intermittently in my late thirties and forties (for mostly matches, hatches and dispatches).

After having Clancy and eventually enrolling her in a Christian school, I made an effort to take her to church on Sundays, but with Paul being pretty much atheist, it was hard to make it a family affair. It wasn't until my fifties when a combination of my dad getting sick, my smoking habit relentlessly gnawing at me and Paul and I hitting a bit of a rough patch, that I felt the need to reconnect with God.

Today, I still say that I'm a *practising* Christian because I haven't got it right yet. This description works well when it comes to faith, but it always makes me nervous when a doctor says they're *practising* medicine.

Personally, I want my doctor to be *nailing* it.

In all seriousness, my relationship with God is something I've been working on since 2005. (Just because you stand in a garage, doesn't mean you're a car. Just because you go to church, doesn't mean you're a Christian.) Aware of the fact that I am not good at being miserable, unhappy, or angry, I've found that my faith gives me the tools I need to be happy and optimistic.

For a long time, I was nervous about expressing my beliefs. I didn't want to rub anyone up the wrong way. I would do pretty much anything for a quiet life and tried to be everything to everyone, but since deepening my faith, I've learnt that being a people-pleaser is not always the best thing for you and it's not always the best thing for someone else either. Eventually, you need to own who you are and what you believe in. That said, I'm not writing this chapter to preach. I'm writing it to share how my faith made saying goodbye to my parents, identifying and conquering my vices and mending my relationship with Paul possible.

When I think about my genetic make-up and try to determine which traits to attribute to Bruce or Audrey McGranger, I'm sure that my love of making people laugh is hereditary and something given to me by my father. It didn't matter if Dad was telling tall tales about his sisters, who, as he'd say, 'were mad as cut snakes' or sticking a breadstick in his ear (no matter how many stars a restaurant had), Bruce knew how to make you laugh to the point of tears.

While Mum didn't have the same desire to be the entertainer, she played a vital role in our family's ecosystem as an engaging audience. Since her name was Audrey, we started lovingly calling her 'Audient'. I inherited her store of Australian turns of phrase that I've managed to sneak into Irene's vernacular. #GawdSaveIreland

As for my addictive nature, well, that came from my father.

When he was diagnosed with oesophageal cancer, we were all devastated, but not surprised. It's difficult to say how long it took for things to get really bad because my parents kept his illness from us for a long time. I knew he was in and out of hospital for a nasty skin cancer he had on his head due to his love of manning the BBQ without a shirt or hat, but would only learn later that it had spread to his oesophagus.

Dad had smoked heavily from a young age until he finally quit at fifty. Now seventy-nine, we knew that roughly thirty-five years of smoking couldn't have been kind to his health and would be hard to come back from. Watching his once acerbic wit and wisdom fade as he struggled to take a breath or swallow food left me feeling completely overwhelmed.

While it was confronting to notice my parents' hair go grey, their confidence making decisions waver and their sudden need for an afternoon nap increase, it was witnessing them lose the strength to crack or laugh at a joke that broke my heart.

Mum was losing her best friend, soulmate and protector. Paula and I were losing our source of light in an often dark world. While Dad's impending death was technically coming at the appropriate time in the circle of life, nothing felt right about it. When he began to rapidly lose weight due to his inability to eat, Mum had to acknowledge that home wasn't the best place for him and accept the doctors' advice to move him into a hospice.

'Your dad's gone into a hospice, but don't worry – it's not just where you go to die,' she said while giving me an update on the phone one afternoon.

I knew she was in denial. I also knew that the way you die from oesophageal cancer is essentially by starvation. Dad would have access to good doctors, the best medicines, and everything else that could keep him comfortable, but the prognosis was terminal.

With a now fourteen-year-old Clancy still at school and Paul typing away on his computer, I took the opportunity to go for a long walk and try to get my head in the right place. It seemed like everything in my world was unravelling at the same time. Dad was dying, Mum was in denial, my daughter was entering those challenging teenage years (I was anticipating payback to be a real bitch), my own smoking habit had increased to a pack a day and the one person who usually made everything seem right (Paul) seemed to be on a different page.

I know some people turn away from religion when life seems off-kilter, but while on this walk, I decided that I needed to talk to God. Over the next hour I sent up prayer requests, expressed my gratitude, vented my frustrations, asked for guidance, pleaded for help, requested a sign and made a commitment to myself and to God that I would spend the rest of my life trying to be the best possible person I could be.

☆ ☆ ☆

In the meantime, Dad's health continued to deteriorate. Knowing his days were numbered, I spent as much time as I could with him. One day I asked him if he would like to speak to someone from the church. While he'd been an altar boy at St Mary's in Waverley, sung proudly in the choir, and taken us to church on Sundays, he'd never openly talked about his faith. However, I'd noticed in recent years that he'd begun attending his local church again. He told me that he'd like to speak to a minister, but asked if he could do so in private.

Thankful I could help, I asked my own minister, Rev Ross Hathway, if he would be able to come and speak with Dad. I remember Ross being extremely busy at the time, but promising to work hard to reorganise his schedule. Much to my delight, he called back and said he could visit Dad that Wednesday.

Eager to meet him there, I rushed from work only to find Ross had arrived early. We ended up meeting in the corridor just as he was leaving. He told me that they had prayed together and discussed a few Bible verses. He left feeling like my dad was in a good emotional place.

This gave me such comfort. When I entered Dad's room, he was resting. I gently placed my hand on his and asked how his chat went. He told me he really enjoyed it and was happy to remember the Bible verse, John 3:16. I left that day feeling proud that I'd mustered the courage and conviction to facilitate that conversation because honestly, even with my own dad, talking about religion made me nervous.

Since I had to work all the next day, I said that I'd see him on Friday night.

On Thursday night, Paula rang to say that Dad had had a bit of a turn and was resting. It'd be better if I came back on Saturday morning.

While driving to the hospice with Paul and Clancy on the Saturday, Paula phoned. Dad had died. I've read that people often wait until their loved ones aren't around or have left the room to take their final breath. I was upset, but I knew it was his time to go. I surprised myself at how calm I remained as I listened to my sister before hanging up to relay the news to Paul and Clancy. This was something I was dreading because I was so worried about how my daughter would react. Just a week before, I found her crying in the hallway. Figuring it was some sort of high school drama, I asked her what was wrong.

'I'm just so sad about Pa,' she said through sniffles.

Unlike Paul and me, Clancy played her emotional cards close to her chest. She's not the warm and fuzzy, touchy-feely type like her parents. This was out of the ordinary. I realised that losing her grandfather was cutting deep. So when I learnt that Dad was truly gone, my main concern was how she'd react. She'd never known death.

I was also worried about Mum. Fearful of her finding out the news while she was alone, Paula had orchestrated a plan to get her to the hospice so we could tell her in person. When she arrived, she was overcome with grief. She went in to see the man she was married to for fifty-six years. Paula and I asked the kids to stay out of the room so Mum could have a moment. Distressed by the site of Dad's bloated belly, she broke down. I could tell that her plan to remain stoic as she had throughout every hardship in her life was no longer possible.

When Clancy, Julia and James went in, I braced for Clancy's reaction, but she held it together. All the grandchildren did. They simply said goodbye to the Pa they had loved so much.

Somehow I was also still holding my emotions in check.

It wasn't until I began to write Dad's eulogy that the waterworks began.

Because Paula lived closer (and had a lot more patience), she made sure Mum was okay during the planning of the funeral. I coordinated with cousins, friends and colleagues to gather the information to begin to put into words what made my dad just so bloody wonderful.

Some people can't deal with writing about their loved ones. For others, that's *how* they deal with it. As I detailed Bruce McGranger's early life, his accomplishments and his character, and began to list the many people whose lives he enriched, I wept, wailed and carried on like a pork chop. (This was clearly my catharsis.)

By the time of the funeral, I had processed so many emotions that I made it through without pulling any of Kim Kardashian's viral cry-faces. I like to think I did my darling dad justice that day. Judging by the amount of people cry-laughing and laugh-crying, I think we sent him on his way in a fitting manner.

While there will never be another Bruce McGranger, it brings me such joy seeing some of his outlandish humour come out in Clancy and Julia, and his tender side in James.

A few weeks later, I made a big decision. My pack-a-day habit had to stop. In the morning, I'd have a cigarette and a cup of tea. After breakfast, another cigarette. Drive to work, cigarette. Lunch, cigarette. Drive home from work, cigarette. Dinner, cigarette(s). You get the picture.

I'd tried and failed to quit twice before: once in Albury and once when Clancy was little. In Albury, I was told I had high blood pressure and would have to give up either the pill or the fags. After trying hypnosis (the hypnotist coughed the whole way through) and nicotine gum (which does not work when you're double fisting a cigarette and asthma inhaler), I gave up the pill instead.

For some reason, my desire to quit felt different this time.

I was definitely going to do it – no ifs, or buts (or puns). A few people at work had been recommending a hypnotist by the name of John Bullock. Ready to give it another go, I booked an appointment and pulled into a parking spot in front of his office the following week. Before getting out, I knew that there was something I needed to do first. I lit a cigarette. Determined for it to be my last (and best), I didn't even roll the windows down as I sucked the life out of that cancer-stick. When I finally reached the filter, I stubbed it out in the car's ashtray, got out and went inside. Here goes.

A good way to describe what it's like being hypnotised is to imagine driving alone on a highway in a car. You know that feeling when you finally get to your destination and you think, *Gee, I don't even remember driving here?* You knew you were aware of other cars on the road, conscious of your speed and would have reacted to the threat of an accident, but your brain was able to enter some sort of autopilot … This is the goal with hypnosis. Once in this state, your hypnotist guides you to somewhere serene, like a pristine beach that fills your lungs with fresh salty air and warms your (sunscreened) skin with just the right amount of (non-UVA/UVB) sunrays.

When you're lost in your mental holiday, they may describe someone walking by smoking a cigarette. Suddenly your pristine beach smells like a Kings Cross bar in the 1980s. For some reason, this scene seemed to work for me. After coming out of my meditation, I was given tools for when smoking-triggers happen and was encouraged to identify them. If you're wondering what a 'smoking-trigger' is, please see the following list:

- Waking up
- Drinking a cup of tea or coffee
- Cooking
- Beginning a meal
- Ending a meal
- Getting in a car
- Driving in a car
- Getting out of a car
- Making a phone call (I think there's an unwritten rule somewhere that you have to smoke while talking on the phone)
- After sex
- Before sex
- (I don't recommend during)

When I left John Bullock's office and opened the car door, I was hit with a wall of stale cigarette smoke. Surprised that I felt repulsed, I wound down every window and drove home trying to cleanse both my lungs and the upholstery.

While nervous about being back in the environments I usually smoked in, my determination to quit made it easy to overcome my desire to smoke. To this day, I'm proud to say I've never failed. I have, however, vividly dreamt about failing. For years I'd fantasise about someone handing me a cigarette or a joint. I'd take a huge puff and then be so mad at myself until I woke up (beyond relieved) and realised it was just a nightmare.

In 2023 I'll turn seventy and I can confidently say that since quitting ciggies, I've felt fitter and healthier than when I was in my thirties. Sometimes people ask me if I'd consider vaping, but I'm not interested. I don't want to inhale anything unless it's laughing gas.

While quitting smoking made my life infinitely better, I don't remember feeling like everything was rainbows and sunshine around this time. I was still grieving for Dad and Paul and I seemed off. There were no arguments or tears, no talk of separation, just a hint of passive-aggressiveness sprinkled on most of our conversations.

To be fair, a lot had changed. For starters, Clancy was now fourteen and didn't need us as much. Since Paul's role in the home had been constant caregiver, I think not being needed as much caused him to re-evaluate how he spent his days. As for me, I was still trying to work through my grief and gain a deeper understanding and acceptance of my faith. Unfortunately, our paths were not intersecting, which made me feel rather alone. Thankfully, this lumpy time in our life didn't last long. I was given some wonderful relationship advice:

Always accept (even if you don't agree), respect, celebrate and protect one another's individuality and solitude.

When I heard these words, something clicked and I remembered *why* Paul and I had always worked so well. We always accepted each other's passions, celebrated each other's wins, and protected each other's pursuits. We just happened to be at a point in our lives where we were confused about what our individual passions and purposes were.

I wrote him a letter assuring him that no matter the hurdles we faced (individually or as a couple), I would never stop loving, celebrating and protecting him.

It's okay if you're not always on the same page (or even in the same library) as your partner. As long as you have a similar taste in books and agree on what the moral of the story should be, you're heading for the right ending.

By 2011, Mum had adjusted to life without Dad, but was beginning to show signs of dementia. She was also as deaf as a post and refused to wear her hearing aids. This was fine when she was home because it helped her sleep through any noisy nearby construction (or a nuclear war), but when we'd take her out in public, she had no idea of just how loud her own voice was.

At a doctor's appointment with Paula one day, an overweight man came into the waiting room. As he settled into a chair and casually picked up a magazine, Mum shouted, 'Isn't it a shame he's so *fat*!' Confident that everyone within a three-mile radius had heard, Paula's embarrassment gland (which is much larger than mine) was in a world of pain.

Another time while at Paul's mum, Flora's, eightieth birthday, her brother aka Uncle Bob (God rest his soul) was supposed to be singing her praises, but was banging on and on instead about war stories. All of a sudden, little old Audrey shouted, 'Oh, God, does this bloke *ever* shut up?' Gauging by the amount of widened eyes and snort-giggles directed our way, pretty much everyone had heard. The good news was I don't think Uncle Bob had because he was deaf as a post too.

One of the scariest things about Mum not wearing her hearing aids was that she couldn't hear us knocking on her door. Most of the time this could be remedied by using our own set of keys or by calling her phone. But on one occasion, Paula didn't have her key for some reason and was knocking and calling and couldn't get into Mum's flat. Frantic, she found a building attendant and got him to open the door for her. Mum was confused and lying in a puddle of urine in the bathroom.

After a few more scary incidents like that and the fact that Mum couldn't remember to hydrate, we took her to a geriatric specialist who did a series of cognition tests to see if she needed to go into respite care. The one I remember most involved the doctor telling her three words that she wanted her to remember: 'chair', 'lion' and 'orange'. After a five-minute chat, the doctor asked my mum to recall the words.

Nothing. Not a single one.

We felt a mixture of sadness and relief when we finally got her into a respite home in Miranda. Relief knowing that we weren't going to find her collapsed alone at home, sadness knowing that our memories would be picked through, packed up and dispersed to friends, family and thrifty Salvos shoppers.

Over the next three years, I'd visit her every other week. Paula, who lived closer, was the constant and was absolutely amazing. Always generous with her time, love and patience, she did so much for Mum during this period.

At the start of 2015, Paula and her crew flew to Greece to visit Peter's side of the family. With Paula overseas, I made an effort to visit Mum more often because she was getting noticeably weaker and less with it by the day. Part of me started to wonder if she needed to move into higher care. I made a mental note to discuss things with Paula when she returned.

I never got the chance.

After taking a Pilates class in Balmain one day, I checked my phone and saw a huge list of missed calls from the respite home. Even though I was panicky and worried about why they had called so many times, I assumed it was just to tell me that Mum had had a fall or that she needed to move to a higher level of care. Once I got on the phone, I was completely taken aback when a nurse broke the news that she had died.

Guilt, confusion and sadness were just a few of the emotions washing over me as I tried to make sense of what had happened. Desperate to talk to Paula, I knew she'd be difficult to reach in Greece, so I ended up calling Paul. Since we only had one car, we decided I'd just drive straight to the respite home. With Clancy at work and Julia studying in the UK, James was the only one in the family who could come with me that day. As he strode in, tears in his eyes, my now thirty-something nephew was just what

I needed to get through this moment. He was so wonderful as he helped me say goodbye to Mum one last time.

Mum's departure from the earth side of life has left me with a lot of unknowns. Because she had dementia, I often wondered if she felt at peace with God or afraid of what would happen. I did bring her a Bible hoping she might flick through it, but don't know if she ever did. Unlike with Dad, where there was time to have a minister come and chat, Mum's death came so suddenly.

While packing up her room, I found a folded note in one of her pockets. I could tell it was written recently, which made it even tougher to read.

Hi Bruce, it's Audrey. Just wondering where you will be tonight. You must know you can sleep here and still go to work in the morning. Give me a ring later.

The thought of my mum (and so many other people) living in such a confused state makes me sad. On one hand, I think dementia is a bit like pneumonia, 'an old man's friend', in that not remembering the names and faces of the ones you loved might make it easier to leave a life once lived. But on the other hand, I think of the overwhelming fear and bewilderment dementia patients feel spending every day confused about who they are, where they are and why people they 'should know' keep coming to visit.

The note she wrote to Dad still breaks my heart to this day, but I'm comforted by the belief that they're both in heaven, sipping wine, singing along to show tunes and laughing – while Bruce acts the goat with a breadstick in his ear.

CHAPTER 16
Unapologetically Me

'Oh my God, you were *hilarious*, you looked like a crash test dummy!' Todd McKenney blurted out for roughly one million viewers to hear.

While these weren't *quite* the words I was hoping for after dancing on national television, I knew in my heart that they were true. When my *Dancing with the Stars* partner, Carmelo Pizzino, spun me through the air in the final episode of the show, I really did feel like a crash test dummy. That said, I also felt wild, free, comfortable, in my element and, for the first time in a long time, unapologetically me. (I was also at peace knowing that people generally can't look away from a car crash.)

For much of my career, Paul had acted as my manager. Since I wasn't bouncing around from job to job, this mostly entailed basic contract negotiations for *Home and Away*. While this was perfectly fine with me, Ada kept raving about her manager, Claire McLennan (now Savage), and said that we should meet up and have a chat. On top of negotiating my deals, Claire could get me side gigs and endorsements.

This is one of the things I love about my cast mates: you rarely get the feeling that there's competition between us. Don't get me wrong, I've worked with some dickheads over the years and there's every chance I've been a dickhead to somebody, but for the most part, people like Ada have never let their own success get in the way of their desire to watch those they respect and admire rise with them.

After sitting down for a meeting and discovering that we got along like a house on fire, Claire became my manager in 2013. One of the first things she asked was what my professional hopes and dreams were. While she knew I was very happy on *Home and Away* and loved doing pantomime over the holidays, she saw opportunities for me to expand my repertoire and wanted to know if there was something specific on my bucket list that she could help me tick off.

As a matter of fact, there was.

'I'd love to be on *Dancing with the Stars*,' I said.

For years I'd watched my co-stars get to cha-cha, foxtrot and tango on the show and had secretly been wondering why the bastards hadn't called me yet. (Okay, so maybe my body didn't scream 'built for ballroom dancing', but still.)

'Leave it with me,' Claire said and grinned.

Six months later I was offered a spot.

As I began my nascent reality TV dance career, I delighted in the fact that I would get to dust off my amateur dancing shoes and spend hour upon hour whirling, twirling, twisting – and sometimes flipping – to some of my favourite songs. I don't know if it was the exposure to my parents' records at a young age, my innate love of musical theatre or the fact that I'd spent so much time with Paul and his muso mates over the years but knowing my part-time gig would involve dancing to songs I love was my idea of a dream job.

Seriously, in my next life, I'm coming back as a triple threat.

Until then, let me take you back to 2014 when I found you can roam well outside of your comfort zone after the age of sixty – and live to tell the tale.

While slightly terrified at the idea of being dressed only in strategically placed fringe, feathers and diamantes, I was confident that I had enough rhythm to proudly shake what my mother gave me (without scaring small children) and was hopeful it would be enough to keep me on TV for at least a few episodes.

My greatest fear (and anyone who has done *DWTS* will tell you this) was being voted off in the first week. My fragile ego simply would not have coped. Like all of my other professional endeavours, while it would be fun to 'win', I was really there just because it looked like a good time. Never in a million years did I think I'd be dancing in the finale against AFL footballer David Rodan ...

But week after week, for some unknown reason, the judges and Australia kept having me back.

I'm not exaggerating when I say that I'm shocked that I am alive and well enough today to even write this chapter, because *DWTS* was the most physically and mentally gruelling thing I have ever done. The unexpected weight loss of seven kilograms was much appreciated, especially after I saw the first promotional images. For some reason, the wardrobe team dressed me in a form-fitting leprechaun-green dress ... which made me look like a dancing zucchini. But by week four, my body had toned up and I no longer resembled something out of the *Soupe Opéra* basket.

Although my torso may have been trim, taught and terrific, my feet resembled those of a murderous eagle prone to snatching lambs from farmland. Every night I'd roll them over frozen water bottles in an effort to stop the rigor mortis. It wasn't until Sal of the *Natural Normans* told me that I needed to be applying heat, not ice, that they finally regained their flexibility.

There was also an injury to my bum that forced us to swap our plan to do the salsa for the Charleston. I have to confess that this injury didn't happen while dancing. No, angry at my cat one day, I tried to bend down to pick him up, which pinged something in my posterior. (I don't know what we were arguing about.)

From having to learn a new language, to getting comfortable 'vocalising' my moves, to trying to make my sore bum (which lives halfway up my back) exude a 'Latin swagger', I can safely say that it *is* possible to teach an old dog new tricks, although you might have to take her out back and put her down after.

Regardless of the fatigue and injuries, it wasn't difficult to keep showing up. While yes, I was dancing because I love a good time, I was also dancing for a very good cause. When the producers had asked me which charity I wanted to support, I knew it had to be Bears of Hope. Ada had lost her son Harrison just a month before. This incredible organisation really rallied behind her and her family to help them get through it. From providing parents with bears they can take home from the hospital to counselling and support groups, Bears of Hope make it easier for families to face the unimaginable.

Each week that I got to stay on the show, my mind went into *Good Will Hunting* equation-solving mode trying to figure out why I'd outlasted Ricki-Lee Coulter or my *Home and Away* co-star Tai Hara. Both of them were much better dancers than me. Maybe they lacked the boofhead appeal that reality TV viewers love so much? (Obviously, I had buckets full.) The only plausible explanation that I could come up with was that I was brave, gung-ho and not afraid to make an idiot of myself.

Regardless of *why* I made it to the finale, it's an experience that I now keep in the same file as doing stand-up comedy and psychedelic drugs. The 'if you have a good first time, it's best not to risk doing it again' one. Also in this file is my promise to never again to talk about my daughter's bowel movements on national television. In an interview with Edwina Bartholomew during the first night of the show, I used one too many descriptive words to explain why Clancy wasn't there to support me … 'She's back in the hotel with a terrible case of the runs!' As soon as it came out of my mouth, I made a mental note to leave Clancy's trysts with gastro out of the spotlight, but as I type this, I can't help thinking, *Oh dear, I'm doing it again.* Sorry, Clancy.

Even though the world tends to believe Ricky Bobby's catchphrase from *Talladega Nights*, 'If you ain't first, you're last', I would have been mortified if I'd won *Dancing with the Stars* because I knew it wouldn't have been because of my dancing. David Rodan was truly extraordinary. When he and his partner, Mel Hooper, did a Bollywood dance, I couldn't tell who was the 'star' and who was the professional. My only issue with coming second is that Ada and Johnny Ruffo love reminding me that they both won.

Fans and journos often ask what my secret is to a long acting career and how I have energy for things like reality TV dance shows. Not wanting to pontificate, I think there are three contributing factors:

1. I believe you should 'live your life, not your age'.
2. I stopped being a people-pleaser.
3. I have an overactive thyroid.

As soon as I started accepting the fact that not everyone is going to like me (and I'm not always going to like them), I was able to find the tools needed to avoid my knee-jerk Red Mist response to confrontation and find peace knowing that what others think of me is really none of my business.

I mentioned earlier that I believe people come into your life for a reason, a season or a lifetime. Over the years I know that certain people have helped me hone the subtle art of not giving a f*ck, while others were my reason for being. (You know who you are.) It's not always clear why, but some people naturally exit once they've taught you the lesson you needed to learn. As for those you thought would be there for a lifetime but weren't – don't underestimate how transformative the season you shared together was.

As I approach the age when many white male politicians enter higher office, I'm aware that some may be wondering about Irene's fate on *Home and Away*. While I wish I could do a big ole #spoileralert, the truth is, I have no idea.

I also feel like COVID-19 has changed my perspective. Like most people in early 2020, when the news of the virus started taking over the media, I didn't know if I was overreacting or underreacting. Surely, this whole thing would blow over quickly, right?

Wrong.

As the months ticked by and the world ground to a halt, production of *Home and Away* stopped, which meant that for the first time in nearly thirty years, I was having an actual break. Unfortunately, this break was due to a global pandemic.

I'd lived through an epidemic once before, but on a much smaller scale when rubella broke out in London in the late

1970s. That time, I wasn't particularly worried and actually caught German measles … which, by the way, partly felt like my mother's fault. You see, my entire youth she tried to get me to catch German measles so my young and strong immune system would develop the antibodies. I think her theory stemmed from the Chickenpox Party Playbook. Regardless, even Mum taking the food out of a sick person's mouth and shoving it in mine didn't work! So there I was at age twenty-five in London: crook as Rookwood.

The worst thing about getting German measles as an adult is that it goes to your joints and affects you in an arthritic way. This meant that it took me roughly forty times as long to do anything. If I hadn't been to the bathroom in a while and anticipated I'd be busting in about thirty minutes, I knew I better start moving. Since I was staying in that cockroach-infested bed and breakfast at the time, someone who'd already recovered (or someone who was about to get it from me) would have to help me out of bed and down the stairs to the communal bathroom.

When I was finally able to grip a phone and numb my throat enough with whiskey, I called to tell Mum I was on death's doorstep. She rejoiced, 'Finally! You'll have the antibodies!'

But I digress … Although I'd lived through an epidemic once before, this time I was in my sixties with a pre-existing health condition (thanks to the fact I was a once-upon-a-time heavy smoker) and really didn't want to catch COVID. I found myself waking every day with a great big knot in my stomach. After having my thyroid biopsied and copious amounts of other blood work done, I can now confidently describe that sensation as anxiety.

Was it having my work routine disrupted?

Was it the fact that I could no longer see Clancy because her boyfriend Luke worked in a front-line job?

Was it my increase in pinot noir consumption?

Who knows. What I do know is that I was able to control these bouts of terror by downloading a few meditation apps and surrendering to the fact that the pause button had literally and figuratively been hit on my work life. And there was nothing I could do about it.

As soon as I was able to accept this, everything calmed down. I stopped and smelled the roses. I began taking the time to read books, listen to podcasts, and clean stuff that didn't even know it needed to be cleaned. First it was the cupboards, next Paul's tequila bottle collection.

In between making the skylights shine brighter than all the *Dancing with the Stars* costumes combined and taking time to call friends and family for long overdue life chats, I began to wonder if maybe I should be spending my remaining years away from Steadicams, stage lights and scripts . . .

But before I could get used to the idea, Australia seemed to get a handle on things. *Home and Away* resumed filming and despite any cough, sore throat or sniffle causing entire storylines to be scrapped and extra filming days added to our six-day-a-week schedule, being back at Summer Bay just felt right.

Sure, part of me missed the downtime, but another part was keenly aware that getting paid to perform alongside people I love and admire (again, you know who you are) brings me great personal fulfilment.

Of course it's fine to not want to stay on a soap forever – most people don't – but for those of us who love going to work on a long-running TV show, the trick is to keep giving the writers a reason to keep writing for you. I think Irene is still kicking around Summer Bay because I'm emotionally invested in her wellbeing and I love her.

Should the show end tomorrow, or should I choose to leave down the track, of course I'd be heartbroken, but I still wouldn't be done yet. If not TV, maybe it'll be another play, a film, a panto production ... another book ... or even manufacturing Irene dolls.

Or maybe it'll just be me acting up on the great stage of life.

Acknowledgements

A huge thanks to everyone at Echo Publishing – Benny, Tegan, Emily and Rosie – for their help and encouragement, and for approaching my manager with the harebrained idea that I write a book.

To my gorgeous, savvy manager, Claire Savage of CMC Talent, who always has my back and takes no shit.

To the extraordinary, talented and hilarious Summer Land, who helped me find my voice and has since become a dear friend.

To all those people – good, not so good or downright hideous – through whose lives I have passed and who have helped shape me (wouldn't have minded a waist and a bum, people!) and given me so much fodder for this book.

To all my many beautiful friends down the ages, who have such a big place in my heart, especially to my besties: Maudie, Kerry, Michelle, Julie and Ada.

To my amazing family, near and far, I love you all, especially the really wacky ones.

To my darling Mum and Dad. I hope you're equal parts delighted and horrified from heaven.

And last, but never least, to my darling Paul and Clancy. Thank you for putting up with me and loving me, even though I repeat myself a lot, I leave cupboard doors open, and I repeat myself a lot. I love you so much. You are my delight and my wild things, you make my heart sing, you make everything groovy. (With thanks to the Troggs!)